One Body Many Illnesses

An Insightful Approach
to Medical Astrology

Alan R. Wheatcroft

Disclaimer: All persons whose cases and charts are discussed and illustrated in this book gave their permission to disclose the relevant details.

ISBN-10: 0-86690-657-6
ISBN-13: 978-0-86690-657-9

Cover Design: Jack Cipolla

Published by:
American Federation of Astrologers, Inc.
6535 S. Rural Road
Tempe, AZ 85283

Printed in the United States of America

Acknowledgements

Thank you…

To my father Robert, for your much-needed support, your wisdom and more importantly for showing me the light in my hours of darkness.

To Sheila, for your inspiration, knowledge and guidance, and more importantly for your love and friendship.

To Alison Huxtable, for your support, your understanding and your empathy, but more importantly for your enthusiasm.

To Wanda Sellar, for your support, your insight and for your vital contribution that has made this book *complete*.

To Betty Gosling, for your friendship, wisdom and insight; but more importantly for teaching me to think 'outside' of the box so to speak.

To Jenny Brook, for your support and your ear, but more importantly for your priceless friendship.

To Dave Bunker, for your valid assistance and understanding. Your timely discovery gave me insight and a new awareness making it the best new deal of all.

To Paul Newman, for your continuing support, your vital input is necessary for my continued progress.

To Nan Geary and all the staff at *The Mountain Astrologer*, for your support, your guidance over the years, but more importantly for believing in me.

To John Green, for your support and for opening the door that allowed me to enter into the world of "astrological acknowledgement."

To Eric Cann, for your friendship and understanding; and for your wisdom and kindness.

To Dulce Bell Bulley, for your friendship and your valuable insight relating to the "Kingdom of Chiron"; but more importantly for allowing me to discover our karmic connection.

To Patricia Walsh, for helping me to heal and therefore relinquish my karmic wounds.

To Roger Woolger, for opening my third eye to the wisdom of karma, god bless, you will be sadly missed on the Earth-plane. I hope you continue your work and more in the heavenly spheres.

To Michael and Jane Reccia and the Band of Light, for bringing through the wisdom, the unconditional love and the eternal light of Joseph.

To Jonathan Cainer, for your intuitive heavenly guidance and for helping me to discover this wonderful gift of astrology.

To Prem Rawat (M), for your love, kindness and the wisdom of your knowledge, and for being my eyes, lighting the way so I could see my long journey ahead.

Contents

Astrology: the Science of the Divine

"Astrology deals with concepts, forces, and symbols that refuse to be pigeonholed by the limitations of the analytical mind, it eludes modern science's attempts to prove or disprove its validity."—*Dovid Strusiner, one of New Zealand's foremost astrologers and founder of the Sacred Astrology movement*

ASTROLOGY, MEANING THE "CELESTIAL LANGUAGE of the cosmos," has been *misunderstood* for the greater part of our collective evolution. Today, we do not *think* in the same lateral capacity as the ancient spiritual civilizations once did; nor do we believe in self-healing as the ancients did, because the simple truth is that no longer are we divinely connected to the physical plane of Earth. In fact, it is fair to say that we give little or no respect to our planet and its long-term spiritual preservation. How then can we be in awe of something that, not only do we perceive as "uninteresting," but cannot fully comprehend? Put simply, astrology is symbolic of a divine purpose. Emanating from its core is an interconnected stellar consciousness that typifies the cosmos as an unprecedented unified entity; and an eminent part of something that is infinitesimal. Moreover, astrology epitomises a universal structure made up of limitless symbolisms.

The science of astrology is an embodiment of creation. So, for example, every symbol in the zodiac represents a separate and consolidated intelligence on the helical of evolution, characterised by the planets and the stars. Hence, the cosmos corresponds as the spiral's internal workings, with the Sun, Jupiter and Saturn at its *heart*. The Sun represents the life force and Jupiter circulates the Sun's energy via the spiral's arterial and responsive systems, which are governed by the innermost planets: Mercury, Venus, Mars and the Moon. Saturn is the timely pulse that beats to the divine influence and pull of the transpersonal masters: Uranus, Neptune and Pluto; whose purpose is to exemplify the power of higher reasoning, incorporeal transcendence and evolutionary ascension.

The ancients believed that we, as humans, emanate from a higher level of consciousness, as indeed we do. Unfortunately, our obsession with *materialism* and other related issues prevents us from realising this heart-warming and reassuring fact. Therefore, we *have* and *continue* to deviate from this universal truth mainly because of the proliferating levels of egotistical idealism that are widespread upon this planet. These concepts are nothing new as they have existed in the minds of men for millennia.

Undeniably, astrology can offer us limitless potential, because the planets provide an innate opportunity (especially when aspected with each other) for individual progression, and for harmonic and cultural development (evolution). In the spirit world thoughts and creativity manifest merely through the application of *light*, or in laymen's terms, electromagnetic energy—the driving force of the universe. On the physical plane (Earth) the manifestation of light energy should also be acknowledged and therefore applied to our daily cycle of progressive learning. Indeed, throughout the centuries our foresight of this universal axiom has been tainted by a myriad of life-altering conditionings. Thus, if modern-day mankind were to become truly connected to Earth and the cosmos, like his ancient ancestors were, the notion of light energy would not only be understood but it would be utilized in a way that it was meant—for the purpose of creativity.

Today, a large percentage of human beings in their current state of disillusionment and perceived ideals, view life merely as a repetitive state of *existence*, and they view it with an "increased density of sight," meaning they are looking through a glass darkly. Putting it another way the effects of the last Earth cataclysm (the destruction of Atlantis 65,000 years ago, to which we are all feeling its effects via difficult planetary alignments) has clouded our creative potential; our observations, our objectivity and our perceptions of how life is meant to be on Earth.

These discernable conceptions have transformed our understanding of the physical universe to which we all inhabit. On Earth, where the application of darkness is the prevalent and widely accepted force, we merely peep at the cosmos through our limited telescopes and other such devices; and our opinions and criticisms are influenced via scientific and religious viewpoints. Rarely do we observe the cosmos through a spiritual conviction.

If the light was turned on again in our souls, and in the Earth soul, the planets would be viewed as crystalline spheres emitting higher harmonic vibrations. These higher harmonic vibrations or intense projections of light energy would emit a specific band or ray of color and each color projection would be conducive to a particular planetary experience. So, for example, the unified and impersonal significators of Venus would be projected on an intense blue/green ray. The ancient astrologers knew these facts all too well.

Astrology is a projection of the superior forces, hence the divine collective will, but similar to the skewed and destructive undertakings of the Earth plane the energies of the spheres have also been tarnished. In other words what we see and experience is not a true reflection of the cosmos and its ultimate purpose.

In effect illness and disease are nothing more than an illusion, hence a projection of thought energy, but they seem very real. We are all capable of healing ourselves, however for the majority of individuals that has become virtually impossible because no longer do we see our body's as vessels of infinite light energy; instead we see our body's as vessels comprising of dense finite matter that succumbs to the process of ageing and disrepair. Similar to our overall views on astrology and other spiritual matters when it comes to our well being all we need to do is change our mindset, it's as simple as that! I hope that by reading the information in this book it will help to change your mindset and your perception of life.

Preface

BOOKS ON MEDICAL ASTROLOGY DO not widely proliferate as do those in other areas of astrology, and Alan's book is therefore especially welcome along with his insights and thoughts. To say that it is a monumental work is no exaggeration, and the task he has undertaken is difficult, but one that has proved its worth in culmination. It certainly appears to bear the fruits of his considerable research and wisdom.

It is not a book for the beginner or indeed anyone who has not the time to read, meditate and analyse the information contained within it. That said, it is written very coherently and simply, and ultimately very readable so it could well appeal across the board.

He shows his knowledge both in traditional astrology and other forms like evolutionary astrology, as well as psychology and past lives. Therefore, it is a book that contains a holistic approach to illness. There are many diverse areas to explore in the study of the body and he endeavours to lead us to their scrutiny. I particularly liked the chapters on the Nodal Axis, which are full of insight. I also was impressed by his description of Retrograde planets and their possible link to illness.

He also assesses biorhythms in relation to the planets and their aspects. He takes us through the meaning of the chakras and their relationship to astrology. They are subjects that of course, merit a deep study.

He gives us many case histories of diverse conditions, and shows how he tackles the problems as an astrologer and healer.

It is a well written and well researched book, but not a light read, which really praises and not blames him.

Wanda Sellar, QHP, DMS. Astrol
Author of An Introduction to Medical Astrology

Introduction

"When health is absent, wisdom cannot reveal itself, art cannot manifest, strength cannot fight, wealth becomes useless, and intelligence cannot be applied."—*Herophilus, Greek physician*

IT IS MY HOPE THAT this book will appeal to a wide range of readers, including both amateur and professional astrologers.

I have developed an efficient system of astrological chart interpretation that can be used in all fields of study, including mundane, traditional, evolutionary and medical astrology. This system incorporates the rulers of the Nodes as the foundation blocks—the beginning of the astrological cycle of life. It is my shared belief that the rulers of the Nodes are the cosmic keys that can unlock the personal vault of knowledge that characterizes the entire chart. The potential and the probable ramifications of the Nodes and their ruling planets have been clearly defined throughout the medical case studies I have chosen to outline in this book. Furthermore, the specific illnesses and diseases I have highlighted represent a small percentage of the physical and psychological afflictions that are most prevalent in the world today. The importance of nodal interpretation is a concept I share with American astrologer Kathy Allan.

Kathy Allan's book, *When World's Collide*, is well worth reading. She takes on a whole new and dynamic perspective in her approach to the definitive purpose of the Nodes. For the most part, and especially throughout modern Western astrology, the interpretations of the Nodes have somehow become *distorted* and *fragmented*. This much-needed book will no doubt help to change this skewed conception.

In addition, I have included some symbolic, biological and spiritual vestiges that are often regarded throughout modern western civilizations and medicine as *undefined*; but they do perform an essential role in the function and maintenance of the body on a daily basis. These vestiges are the lunar biorhythms and the solar chakras, both of which have a profound effect on the astrological influences that continually affect our lives. Furthermore, the biorhythms and chakras play a significant role in the onset of illness—the ancient astrologers were aware of this fact centuries ago.

Portraying these influences as an important part of the horoscope has been achieved in part by ascertaining their positions via the archetypes (signs) and the hierarchies (planets). To help better understand this rudimentary form of chart interpretation I have backed up my findings with the appropriate case study, and one that is clearly relevant to chakra malfunction, and biorhythm depletion, which occurs during times of difficult planetary transits.

According to Louise Hay "all symptoms of illness and disease are messages from the Higher Aspects of the psyche." In fact, if we identify further with the word disease and hyphenate it, hence "dis-ease," therein lies a big clue to the meaning of illness. Currently, the increasing worldwide opinion, especially amongst spiritual healers, is that illness is necessitated when the soul is *inadvertently* diverted from its ordained path of evolutionary progression.

Illness and disease are preordained. Therefore, they are initiated by the intricate dynamics that are at work within the body; hence the spiritual, physical and the psychological interplay between the planets, the biorhythms and the chakras. In essence what are termed as "minor ailments" begin with a physical impairment or disposition such as catching a cold or the flu and as a result these minor ailments create an energy imbalance in the body. The catalysts for creating these bodily imbalances are often referred to as aggravants—everyday stresses and strains. Aggravants manifest as overwork, exhaustion and emotional and psychological stress; for example the person who works a seventy-hour week will have a depleted immune system. An improper diet also will play a significant role in the onset of illness.

Investigations have revealed that the current epidemic of social addiction to alcohol, referred to as "binge drinking," will have catastrophic consequences on the health of those who consistently partake in this dangerous endeavor. It is a fact that binge drinking depletes the immune system, thus inhibiting the flow of energy around the body, which in turn destabilises the chakras, causing damage and affliction to the major organs such as the heart, kidneys, and liver. Liver and kidney disease, kidney stones, gallstones, pancreatitis, heart disease, and even cancer are all physical provocations associated with alcohol abuse.

Minor illness and disease is essentially an early warning sign; and minor illness will only proliferate if an individual *refuses* to acknowledge that innovation and transformation are crucial life components that are necessary for the evolutionary progression of the soul. These fundamental factors become especially relevant when transiting Uranus, Neptune, and the generational planet Pluto become a prevalent and commanding force in the birth chart, and more so if the warning signs of minor illness is already evident.

If an improper diet is the cause of illness I would immediately suggest embracing a healthier option. Visit a nutritionist for advice; moreover, acquire as much information on nutrition as you can because however many conscious or unconscious choices are made where nutrition is concerned the body will always react accordingly to them (there is a particularly good website address in the final chapter of this book). Remember, the body is a separate unified intelligence that it is totally aware of our thoughts and actions. Essentially, we are what we eat! Unacknowledged, the symptoms of minor illnesses will transmute into *major* illness and at that point the termination of the life plan may become a realistic possibility.

All forms of illness and disease involve the biorhythms and

the chakras. When an individual consciously or unconsciously breaks the conditions that are written into the universal contract, so to speak the *agreed* soul path, the potential for illness becomes an ever-increasing possibility, and in many cases a harsh reality. Illness can also be an inherent condition from past lives—some unfinished business perhaps; it can also be genetic. But in ninety percent of all cases illness and disease manifest as a direct result of our actions, and these actions are evoked by a heavily-conditioned lifestyle, coupled by our unfettered engrained notion of free choice.

In retrospect, we must try to remember that free choice should not be taken literally or in the loosest sense of the word. Free choice, which is the fundamental law of the physical universe is a precursor or forerunner that injects awareness into the heart of our divine plan, meaning that free choice manifests as an instinct or an intuition telling us that when something feels right it feels right *per se*. Essentially, free choice offers us the potential to differentiate between right and wrong, and every individual on the face of this Earth *knows* the difference between right and wrong.

Because the chakras represent the Higher Aspects of the psyche this is where, in effect, illness and disease manifest from. When illness and disease pervade our lives, the Higher Aspects notify the chakras instructing them to reduce their energy output. Consequently, this energy drain orchestrates a malfunction within the organ or organs they oversee. Hence, this underlying problem occurs when transiting planets align to natal positions, angles and midpoints. The biorhythms will also be affected as they are naturally connected to the chakras. This early warning stage of energy depletion corresponds with the holistic term: being out of balance. However, if the cause of the illness is quickly realized and thus corrected, the chakras will begin restoration by realigning their energy vortex, wherein the organs are replenished with energy and the illness subsides. However, as often is the case, some form of treatment will be required to assist with the healing process—medical or otherwise.

Unfortunately, very few astrologers have studied the effects of the biorhythms and the chakras in the birth chart. However, through serious study of these energy points and waves we could easily facilitate a prevention plan that would effectively *counteract* any potential health problems; in other words, it would be wise to recommend some form of healing that would potentially deter the unpleasant ramifications of illness and disease.

So, for example, if the biorhythms are affected by transiting planets it would be prudent to keep a low profile during that period; moreover be *still*, and begin or increase your program of guided meditations. More importantly, do not apply any additional stress to the body through over-excertion or over-indulgence. It is because of these early warning systems that the chakras and the biorhythms are, without doubt, an important and integral part of medical astrology. Speaking purely as a matter of fact, the biorhythms and the chakras are energy conduits that support and enhance the body's immune system; therefore they could easily be ascertained as the *modus operandi* of the entire birth chart.

Similar to the signs of the zodiac, chakras represent important foundational points, meaning that they integrate their energy with the signs. Working in close proximity to the signs, chakras strengthen and galvanize the outer rim or wheel of the birth chart. In esoteric terms the outer rim represents the HA—Higher Aspects of the psyche—whereas the inner rim or wheel represent the LA—Lower Aspects of the psyche. The houses represent *opportunity* and *potential*, whereas the planets represent necessary *progression*. The houses and the planets are also the key factors in medical astrology because they determine how illness and disease manifest. In my opinion the biorhythms and the chakras must not be overlooked as they invariably signify the art of *prevention* as opposed to the more accepted notion of *cure*.

Alan R. Wheatcroft

Part I

Biorhythms and Chakras

CHAPTER 1

Introduction to Medical Astrology

Give a man a pill, and you mask his symptoms for a day. Teach him to meditate and he can heal his life.

THE RENOWNED HERBALIST AND PHYSICIAN Nicholas Culpeper (1616-1654) used the techniques of astrology alongside his herbal medicines. The birth chart would be used for the diagnosis and Culpeper would treat the illness appropriately. He wrote, "Only astrologers are fit to study medicine and a medicine man without astrology is like a lamp without oil."

Traditional Factors

Medical astrology is an ancient medical system that associates various parts of the body, diseases, and drugs as being under the influence of the Sun, Moon, and planets, along with the twelve astrological signs. Each of the astrological signs (along with the Sun, Moon and planets) is associated with different parts of the human body—the underlying basis for medical astrology. According to the ancients, a planet posited in a particular sign can indicate a weakness, which subject to the correct conditions, can manifest into injury, illness, and even fatality. It largely depends on the aspects between the planets in the natal chart and the transits triggering them.

The primary function of medical astrology is to provide indications as to whether the cosmic influences extant at the time of an illness are likely to be advantageous or disadvantageous to the individual; therefore, medical astrology operates on these four essential points:

- The likely severity of the particular disease.

- The likely duration of the disease.

- The eventual and probable outcome of the disease.

- Any additional means that might be employed by a physician to counteract the disease and thus facilitate the restoration of the patient's health.

Traditionally, the most common astrological methods used in medical astrology are transits and horary astrology. A medical horary chart is also known as a decumbiture chart, as it is normally cast for the time the individual takes to his or her bed, so to speak. Transit charts have only come into use recently and decumbiture charts are by far the most ancient approach.[1]

The Astrological Influences and Effects

Medical astrology teaches us that each planet provides a unique influence with regards to the outcome of an illness; this of course is dependent on the location of the planet in the chart and its position in the zodiac. Correspondently, the signs of the zodiac represent different parts of the physical body, and one or more organs and their functions. Moreover, there are certain very simple principles in astrology that you should master. For example, the mutable signs relate to tuberculosis and mental illness such as dementia; the fixed signs can, among other things, relate to cancer; and the cardinal signs relate to the formation of tumors. In addition, it is reasonable to assume that death can be predicted when the Sun, Moon, and Ascendant are all afflicted by other planetary forces. The houses or quadrants represent environmental or *mundane* influences or effects. Important astrological considerations to be taken into account when performing a diagnosis are as follows:

Aries: relates to the cerebrum, eyes, face, upper jaw, carotid arteries, and front of the body.

Taurus: relates to the larynx and throat, ears, lower jaw, and cerebellum.

Gemini: relates to the neck, collar bone, lungs, bronchi, trachea, shoulders, arms, and sympathetic nervous system.

Cancer: relates to the breasts, diaphragm, oesophagus, taste receptors, and left side of the body.

Leo: relates to the heart metabolism, vena cava, back, spinal cord, and thymus gland.

Virgo: relates to the intestines, duodenum, pancreas, solar plexus, abdomen, and parasympathetic nervous system.

Libra: relates to the kidneys, adrenal glands, loins, lumbar region, and back of the body.

Scorpio: relates to the bladder, urethra, genitals, testes, prostate[2], sigmoid colon, pubic bone, and nose.

Sagittarius: relates to the hips, thighs, femur, sacrum, coccyx, blood vessels, sciatic nerves, and pituitary.

Capricorn: relates to the knees, bones, joints, parathyroids, and in co-rulership with the Sun, the right side of the body.

Aquarius: relates to the lower legs, ankles, circulation, oxidation, and pineal body.

Pisces: relates to the feet, toes, thalamus, and blood fibrin.

Sun: this primary luminary relates to heart function, the spine, and life force energy.

The Moon: this secondary luminary relates to the emotions, fluid retention, hormones, stomach, digestive system, lymphatic system, and the mucus membranes.

Mercury: relates to the central nervous system, brain, thyroid gland, hands and fingers, and the five senses.

Venus: relates to nutrient assimilation, sugar metabolism, tissue tone, lymphatic function, thymus gland, sense of touch, and ovaries.

Mars: relates to the sex drive, organ metabolism, muscle function, adrenal glands, and the senses of smell and taste.

Jupiter: relates to the arteries, blood circulation, liver and fat metabolism, cellular nutrition, and the pituitary gland.[3]

Saturn: relates to the body's natural defenses, spleen, hair, teeth, and skin; Saturn is connected with bodily neglect.

Uranus: relates to the parathyroid gland, neural activity, and the aura, and also begets spasm; Uranus is connected to the body's hypersphere.

Neptune: relates to poisons, the pineal gland, and all forms of psychic healing. During Neptune transits, especially when the luminaries are involved, this planet indicates that *vitality* is leaking from the body. Neptune is connected to the soul chakras.

Pluto: relates to pancreatic function, the body's metabolism, elimination, and the pituitary gland. Pluto is the planet associated with higher brain function and the biorhythms.

The houses are also a significant and important factor in medical astrology; however in a decumbiture chart (a chart for the onset of an illness or "when the patient takes to his bed," the attention is mainly focused on these five houses:

Ascendant/first house: representing the patient's body, general health, and vitality.

Sixth house: representing the patient's disease or injury and acute health problems.

Seventh house: representing the judgment of the physician or the person attending the patient.

Eighth house: signifying the patient's death and the place of longevity.

Tenth house: signifying remedies that are necessary or appropriate.

The planetary rulers of the houses are the significators of medical factors and events. Originally, only the seven traditional planets—Sun, Moon, Mercury, Venus, Mars, Jupiter, and Saturn—were used in medical astrology. However, I use all ten planets and all twelve houses because doing so provides a much clearer definition of the nature of the problem.

Following is the medical importance of the remaining houses:

Second house: relates to the blood vessels and the nerves that connect to the throat and neck.

Third house: relates to the intake of air and the breath that sustains the life force energy.

Fourth house: relates to last phase of life and the functioning of the gastric and digestive systems.

Fifth house: relates to the body's overall equilibrium and the interplay between the chakras.

Ninth house: relates to the functioning of the body's arterial system and the nervous system.

Eleventh house: relates to the circulation of the blood around the body and the place of the mind, body, and soul.

Twelfth house: relates to the lymphatic system, the place of death and hospitalization, chronic health problems, and the unconscious state, such as sleep.

Dignities

Dignities are extremely important components in medical astrology; therefore, to be able to make a successful diagnosis it is important to understand the system of dignities. Dignities are divided into two categories referred to as essential dignity and exaltation, and detriment and fall. A planet posited in either of the first two categories is considered strong, whereas a planet posited in either of the latter two categories is considered weak.

For example, if the Moon is in Capricorn (in its detriment) and is found making a tight inconjunction to Uranus in Leo (also in detriment), both these planets would be considered as weak and would therefore undermine the houses of the chart they occupy. If diagnosis were necessary, this single aspect would play a major role toward the onset of potential illness, providing of course that there are other significators present.

Primary Indicators

Energy levels and general health factors are determined by the condition of the Sun, which is symbolic of the life force and overall vitality. Emotional and psychological well-being are determined by the condition of the Moon, which is symbolic to the general flow of the life force energy. Aspects, including detrimentations and falls between these planets and with the Ascendant ruler, especially aspects from Mars, Saturn, and Pluto, indicate a *weakening* in the overall levels of vitality. The eastern hemisphere of the chart (Ascendant side) can often indicate a weakening in the left side of the body, depending on the effects of aspects and planetary dignities. The western hemisphere (Descendant side), sometimes referred to as the oriental side, can indicate a weakening in the right side of the body. Below is a list of the planets in dignity:

Essential Dignity	Detriment
Sun in Leo	Sun in Aquarius
Moon in Cancer	Moon in Capricorn
Mercury in Gemini	Mercury in Sagittarius
Venus in Taurus	Venus in Scorpio
Venus in Libra	Venus in Aries
Mars in Aries	Mars in Libra

Introduction to Medical Astrology

Jupiter in Sagittarius
Saturn in Capricorn
Uranus in Aquarius
Neptune in Pisces
Pluto in Scorpio

Jupiter in Gemini
Saturn in Cancer
Uranus in Leo
Neptune in Virgo
Pluto in Taurus

Exaltation

Sun in Aries
Moon in Taurus
Mercury in Virgo
Venus in Pisces
Mars in Capricorn
Jupiter in Cancer
Saturn in Libra
Uranus in Scorpio
Neptune in Cancer
Pluto in Aries

Fall

Sun in Libra
Moon in Scorpio
Mercury in Pisces
Venus in Virgo
Mars in Cancer
Jupiter in Capricorn
Saturn in Aries
Uranus in Taurus
Neptune in Capricorn
Pluto in Libra

Retrogrades

Retrograde planets are considered to be more difficult in medical astrology, especially when Saturn, Neptune, and Pluto are highlighted, because these planets can be attributed to chronic illness.

When Mercury is retrograde and in hard aspect to other planets, particularly by way of sesquiquadrate or inconjunction, and especially to the luminaries, which is relevant to all retrogrades, there may be a slowing down of nerve signals and thyroid activity. However, chronic diseases such as multiple sclerosis may *relapse* during a transiting phase of retrograde Mercury. Further, symptoms of reduced vision caused by optic nerve delay could increase along with delayed bladder function and other delayed motor-sensory responses.

When Venus is retrograde there is a tendency to activate genetic diseases; the kidneys are inclined to store these inherent tendencies. Venus retrograde related illnesses may appear refractory and difficult to clear; but in the long-term a cure may be found. Moreover, Venus related illness requires the use of suitable remedies to ultimately *clear* the inherited condition. Childhood weaknesses in the kidneys may also reappear during retrograde phases and manifest as, for example, suppressed ear infections. Another affliction for a natal retrograde Venus is a weakness in the kidney reproduction system; this has been caused by the over-indulgence of unregulated sex in past lives that led to infection caused by a sexually transmitted disease.

When Mars is retrograde, past life and current life injuries may reappear, and there can be the onset of muscular pain, often without an obvious connection to any injury. Blood disorders such as haemophilia, blood clots in the brain, and blood poisoning are also a factor when Mars is or turns retrograde, especially when making hard aspects to Saturn or Neptune. Haemophilia is an hereditary and karmic disposition.

When Jupiter is retrograde, metabolic and liver diseases may be activated; this is also the result of causation from past lives. Symptoms of gluttony can reappear; if so, the liver will suffer from over-use. This can sometimes relate to blood deficiency caused by the depletion of enzymes and bile juices. Also, the liver can be damaged because of stagnation and toxicity caused by retained food and alcohol products. Further, the body is prone to losing heat during a Jupiter retrograde phase because the liver regulates the body's temperature. Heat depletion occurs because the liver is hard-pushed to clear the toxic waste that has accumulated in the body.

When Saturn is retrograde it may appear difficult to attain and retain any sense of optimism, especially upon the healing journey of life. Behavioral and habitual patterns may keep repeating and thus lead to the onset of disease. Also, illness and disease are likely to linger to the point of permanence. Rigidity can also affect the muscular and skeletal systems, causing arthritis and rheumatism; this is because the ego has become *fixated* with stereotypical beliefs, ideas, and perceptions about life.

When Uranus is retrograde, intense patterns of nerve-muscle cramping are likely because the signals sent from the brain to the rest of the body have become delayed or obstructed. Depending on relevant issues in the birth chart, when Uranus turns retrograde or is retrograde, epileptic-type fits can also develop. A retrograde Uranus can also indicate that in past lives psychic abilities and other powers of the mind were abused, causing a confused mind unable to manifest ideas into action.

When Neptune is retrograde there is a hidden mass of psychic karma present that has amassed from an abuse of power or responsibility in past lives. This is particularly relevant from those early lifetimes on ancient Atlantis. In this life a retrograde Neptune will manifest in the psyche as oppression or extreme negativity and psychic meltdown. Problems in the lymphatic system can also arise.

When Pluto is retrograde there may be buried and painful soul parts trapped in the underworld and subconscious realms that persistently cause disease. In order for the body to heal, the soul parts need to be integrated back into the whole or body's energy field. If left unchecked the trauma will be felt in the abdominal centres.[4]

The Causes of Illness

According to the dowser and spiritual healer Uta Rogers there are seven physical causes of illness and disease, which are as follows:[5]

- Neglect
- Congestion
- Trauma

- Chemical, Metal and Environmental Toxins
- Infection
- Parasites
- Miasma and the Residue of Childhood Diseases

Using Uta's premise, let us now look at how these causes can manifest as potential problems in the body.

Neglect

This is primarily associated with food intake such as improper food choices and combinations. A further example of neglect would be associated with the body's intake of proteins, carbohydrates, fats, vitamins, minerals, and the all-important essential fatty acids. Neglect can also include the misuse of diet plans, meaning being on a specific plan that is correct and not one that necessarily suits the pocket or looks good in promotional advertising. The consumption of water is also an important factor; drinking the correct amount and the right kind is imperative—distilled, mineral or spring, alkalized or magnetized, whatever is right for your body. Neglect is frequently orchestrated because of afflictions between the Sun, Moon, Venus, and Neptune.

Congestion

It is a well-known medical fact that many diseases begin with congestion in the body. Pain can also be associated with congestion. Likewise, an organ or gland, muscles or bones, can all be affected by congestion. Stagnation is also a form of congestion. The most prolific kind of stagnation is associated with the liver and this can cause depression and mood swings. The liver is responsible for digestion, hormone balance, cleansing the blood, and stabilization of the blood sugars. It is also a fact that many people suffer from congestion of the liver, especially in Western cultures where the consumption of fried food is all too common. Liver congestion invariably affects the gall bladder and gall bladder ducts; this is the main cause of gallstones and associated illnesses such as pancreatitis. Congestion is caused through afflictions between the Sun, Moon, Jupiter, and Saturn.

Trauma

It is widely believed that trauma is one of the most misunderstood and undiagnosed causes of ill health today. Trauma can be brought on by many issues such as the loss of someone close to us, the loss of a job, an accident, anything that causes the trauma to become *internalized* in the body. Therefore, trauma must be treated as a chronic condition purely and simply because it affects the day-to-day momentum of life. As in many cases trauma can also manifest as a direct result of neglect in childhood. Trauma can affect the general health of an individual in ways that are totally unknown because trauma is stored in the body's cellular memory, thus affecting the overall condition of each individual cell. Trauma comes in many guises that manifest through the physical, emotional, and psychological pathways, and if not addressed correctly, illness and disease will arise as a result. Trauma is highlighted when the Sun, Moon, Mercury, Mars, Uranus, and Pluto are afflicted.

Chemical, Metal and Environmental Toxins

There are a myriad of manufactured chemicals in the world today, many of which are used on a daily basis. Unfortunately, when chemicals enter the body and are not excreted via the body's natural channels they can create a reaction in the body called "multiple chemical sensitivity," and this condition is categorized as an environmental illness. Environmental illnesses are essentially allergic reactions to environmental patterns and events. Environmental illnesses are not easy to define until an understanding is developed between the chemical intoxication and the symptoms of the illness. However, symptoms often range from breathing difficulties, lapses in memory, and fogginess in the brain. These sensitivities can all occur after exposure to harmful chemicals and heavy metals, especially when oxygen depletion occurs because of "poor air." Symptoms can be set off by inhaling detergents, by a visit to the dry cleaners; also by inhaling car exhaust fumes, even being in a newly-decorated living or office space. The main affliction arising from multiple chemical sensitivity is depression, and therefore can be evident when there are afflictions between the Sun, the Moon, Mars, Neptune and Pluto.

Infection

Colds and flu are classic common examples of infection. There are many other kinds of infection that can frequent the body, including more than ninety viruses, all of which are from the herpes virus family. Mostly, all kinds of infection fall into two categories: *bacterial* and *viral*. However, infections of the herpes virus family range from skin eruptions, cold sores, and shingles to chronic fatigue syndrome, or fibromyalgia. Other infections include Candida, which is a kind of fungal infection, and tick borne illnesses such as Lyme Disease. Fungal infections are common and can invade the body and inhabit the outer areas of the glands, muscle tissue, and organs. Sometimes it is difficult to remove a particular virus unless other viruses and fungi are removed first. Infections occur in the body when the Sun, Moon, Venus, or Saturn are afflicted.

Parasites

Parasites are tiny creatures that can cause a multitude of problems in the body. Some parasites such as worms are visible to the human eye, whereas others are not so visible. Visible parasites include tapeworms, roundworms, pinworms, hookworms, and flukes. Microscopic parasites of the protozoan genus group include amoebas and cryptosporidiums, which are shape-shifting organisms. Essentially, parasites deprive the body of nutrition and excrete their toxic waste into the body. Severe parasite infections are frequently associated with a weak digestion, an overburdened liver, and a debilitated kidney function.

Symptoms of parasitic invasion include the following: diarrhoea, allergy, constipation, anaemia, gas and bloating, IBS (Irritable Bowel Syndrome), fatigue, immune system dysfunction, sleep disturbances, and mood swings. Parasites invade the body when the Sun, Moon, Uranus, Neptune, or Pluto are afflicted.

Miasma and Childhood Diseases

A miasma is an *inherent* condition that emanates from the ancestral gene pool to which it creates physical debilitation in the body. A primary example of a miasma is spinal deformity, which can be an after-effect of tuberculosis. All diseases are in fact manifestations of a miasma. If childhood afflictions are still evident in adulthood it is often due to the residue from vaccines or from diseases such as chicken pox, mumps, diphtheria, rubella, polio, and small pox. Miasmas occur when the Sun, Moon, Venus, Mars, Saturn, Uranus, or Pluto is afflicted.

Finally, as this is not a book that touches specifically on the traditional practices of medical astrology, I would instead like to begin my overall analysis by touching on something that has a profound and significant effect on our everyday lives, and indeed on medical astrology, and yet it still hasn't been fully accepted as a recognized or influential force: the body's *hypersphere*, the spiritual mainframe.

Endnotes

[1] Information supplied by Wikipedia.

[2] Prostate Cancer is increasing in the UK and parts of Europe. This is partly because of a lack of detoxification in the body caused by increasingly inadequate levels of sunshine, which kills fungus in the body. This is related to a marked increase in precipitation due to the shifting jet stream.

[3] A reference in conjunction with Robert Carl Jansky's book *Astrology Nutrition and Health* published in 1977, to which he states that Pluto "may be the ruler of the pituitary gland." This is

the master gland that controls growth, hormonal secretion, and the development of the secondary sex characteristics at puberty. In my opinion this organ is ruled by both Jupiter and Pluto as both planets seem to fit the bill well so to speak. With Pluto ruling hormones and with its polarity planet, Venus, ruling sex and Jupiter ruling growth (the expansion of matter and spirit) the pituitary gland most definitely falls under these planetary rulerships. For growth to occur, all these bodily secretions need to be delivered to designated areas within the body and that is where Jupiter's polarity planet Mercury comes in—the messenger.

[4]The effects of retrogrades in medical astrology are described by Prashna Kundali.

[5]Uta Rogers works as a vibropath. For more information about her work go to www.utarogers.com

CHAPTER 2

The Body's Hypersphere

"Astrology is the blueprint of the forces that flow into
the body and maintain it."—William M. Davidson, MD

ENVELOPED AROUND THE PHYSICAL BODY is an aural energy-field, or hypersphere, meaning "body of light." The ancient alchemists and shamans believed the universe was essentially one monumental hypersphere—essentially a doughnut-shaped object that is representative of the scientific concept known as four-dimensional space. In addition, Earth is surrounded by its own unique and translucent hypersphere.

This multidimensional shape-shifting light transfiguration is comprised of twelve meridian-like channels or energy fields.[1] Conceptually, we can hypothesize that these energy fields symbolize the twelve signs of the zodiac—the twelve metabolic states—that are archetypes that process and coordinate information throughout the body that is then expressed and brought into consciousness by the planetary bodies. In retrospect, the overall health and vitality of the body and the life force energy is dependant upon the correct flow and communication of information through these channels. Impasses occur in the life force energy when transiting planets align to natal positions, thereby creating drama, tension, and dilemma. These personalized characteristics become especially relevant when squares, oppositions, sesquiquadrates, and inconjunctions are highlighted.

Maintaining a harmonious connection between the body's biochemistry (the signs) and the bioenergetics (the planets) is crucial at all times and must be facilitated in order to nurture and enhance our physical, psychological, and spiritual well-being. Random and undignified thought patterns, which are primarily orchestrated by difficult planetary alignments, especially oppositions, create an *unregenerate* stream of energy in the body. This in turn necessitates a severing of the link between the flow of information; therefore, the onset of illness is inevitable.

Hyperspheric Sequences

The body's hypersphere begins at the top of the skull (the higher crown chakra and the North Node) and travels down the spinal column to the base of the feet (the South Node), and pulsates away from the base chakra in an upward motion. Similar to the electromagnetic pulsations of the Earth's new energy grid, which was installed in May 2000, the hypersphere resonates at around 96.2 cycles a second. In addition, the hypersphere has a profound influence on the body's DNA sequences, which resonate at 100 cycles per second.[2]

Moreover, the hypersphere is encoded with microscopic gene sequences that signify unique opportunities for evolutionary growth and progression. However, if these sequences are not correctly interpreted, meaning that if the opportunities for growth are not acted upon and fulfilled, they will remain motionless and inactive. Ultimately, the likelihood is that they will *transmute* into illness and disease, especially illnesses of an inherent nature that are genetically adopted from the family gene pool.

The hypersphere has been encoded with karmic energy patterns and mental confabulations that remain *active* throughout the course of a single incarnation, but because they are not immediately evident they often remain impassable. Furthermore, it is important to remember that the soul is initially rendered *incapable* of discovering its evolutionary purpose until we as hu-

The Body's Hypersphere

man beings successfully purge this karmic energy field, which is engrained in the memory pathways of the hypersphere. In order to do this we need to wake up from our long karmic slumber that we continue to languish in. Hasn't the evolutionary alarm clock gone off yet? Working closely with the Nodes will help us to purge the karmic energy field.

Essentially, the hypersphere can be healed and successfully *maintained* through the simple acts of love, compassion, and forgiveness; it can also be preserved simply by embracing the supernal light of unconditional love. Empowerment by the supernal light will also protect us from those human failings that we incorporate into our daily lives—the actions we commit without *thinking* and that require high levels of unconsciousness and unawareness, both of which have disastrous consequences on the hypersphere. But every time we generate love, compassion, and forgiveness the hypersphere is automatically *reenergized* with universal energy, which is the perfect tonic for every type of illness and disease.[3]

Hyperspheric Infraction

Once illness and disease become a pervading force in the body the hypersphere becomes disorientated, disfigured and in some cases *fragmented*. This disorientation factor is a key element in hyperspheric infraction because it indicates the condition of the soul, as it experiences extensive stress and discomfort. If the soul has undergone fragmentation, it will be clearly shown in the hypersphere.

Alternatively, try to imagine the Earth's hypersphere at this difficult time in our evolution. Instead of looking energized and *vibrant*, it appears jagged, monotonous, passionless, and apathetic. In fact, due to the current levels of sublime illusion and the proliferating levels of ignorance, people still perceive the Earth to be this familiar glowing blue ball, especially when it is viewed from the depths of space. Unfortunately, this is an illusion because the truth paints a very different picture when viewed from the spiritual plane. Sadly, from this dominion the Earth looks like a burnt cinder, distorted and in pain, which indicates the true condition and health of our planet.[4]

Human Health

It is a fact that for us to feel *complete* the hypersphere must remain "whole" and avoid fragmentation at every step upon the journey of life. The hypersphere is a true reflection of our soul. Today, many past-life therapists use guided techniques such as regression therapy and on occasion they are used to *reinstate* soul fragments placing them back at the source. Distressing events that occurred in past lives cause the soul to become traumatized and as a result the soul becomes fragmented and parts of it become dislodged and therefore *trapped* within the passage of time. Not only do humans need to repair their souls and thus heal their individual hypersphere in order to stave off ill health, we also need to discover sacred means by which we can transmit divine light into Earth as a way of healing and restoring Earth's equilibrium, hence reestablishing the planet's hypersphere back to good health. Soul fragmentation occurs when an individual suffers mass trauma, i.e. a serious illness either in a past life or in the present one. Consequently, this damaging effect can leave a lasting impression on the integrated infrastructure of the hypersphere.

The hyphersphere's twelve meridian-like channels or energy fields are each symbolized by a specific color—the colors that represent the signs of the zodiac and their rulership planets. So, for example, if physical incarnation was terminated in a previous life because of a brain tumor, the color red symbolizing Aries and the color yellow symbolising Gemini would cause the energy fields of the hypersphere to appear distorted and the colors would be out of synchronization with each other, meaning some would look superior and others would seem less prominent.

The Body's Hypersphere

Once the hypersphere becomes distorted it is no longer able to create its traditional confluence of color—one that is equally balanced and pulsates via ever-changing spectrums. Alternatively, if the individual died of colon cancer, the color violet symbolized by Scorpio and the metallic hue of silver symbolized by Cancer would once again make the color spectrum appear distorted.

By examining the hypersphere we can tell immediately whether there is a blockage that needs to be cleared or if there is one (or more) that is currently forming in the body. It is through the appearance of the hypersphere with its individual and intermixed colours that holds the key to the body's health. Unfortunately, this ancient hyperspheric premise is yet another long-forgotten and significantly important construct of our being that emanates from the human design pool of intelligence—our angelic roots.

Healing and Prevention

If soul fragmentation has occurred, the colors that represent the particular illness or trauma will be completely *missing* and thus will be absent from the hypersphere, especially if they are colors that are normally *intermixed*; then the hypersphere will simply not display them as part of its luminescent matrix. This process can often be determined simply by examining the condition of the rulers of the Nodes via their aspects and in particular their relationship to the chakras in the birth chart because the chakras signify the colors of the hypersphere. In order to view the hypersphere and also to discover any potential damage, all we need do is look deep within ourselves via the third eye chakra for the answers. This can be done through guided meditation and color therapy.

Furthermore, to prevent further infractions occurring in the hypersphere we must live our life in a conscious manner; for example, learning to be flexible, non-judgmental, and spiritually-minded. Also, we need to prioritize the universal discipline known as unconditional love, meaning we must learn to love ourselves and others through the power of acceptance; we need to learn to forgive, most notably ourselves. Working with colors through visualization therapy is also a good idea, especially when it comes to maintaining the health of the hypersphere. But more important, getting to know the basic teachings of *astrology* will assist greatly in maintaining a healthy equilibrium and thus prevent further trauma that one day you might have to resolve at some distant point on the wheel of time.

Above all else the important thing to remember here is that the hypersphere is the *sustainer* of the soul's energy and the *indicator* of the soul's well-being. Remember this simple premise and you won't go far wrong in your understanding of the simple and beautiful reality we call life.

Below is a list of the hyperspheric colors and hues that symbolize each spiritual DNA strand that represents an important individual compilation and collective piece of the hypersphere:

- Red (Aries/Mars)
- Emerald Green/White (Taurus/Venus)
- Pale Yellow (Gemini/Mercury)
- Silver (Cancer/Moon)
- Gold (Leo/Sun)
- Deep Yellow (Virgo/Chiron)
- Petrol Blue (Libra/Vesta/Dark Moon?)
- Violet/Black (Scorpio/Pluto)
- Purple (Sagittarius/Jupiter)
- Petrol Green (Capricorn/Saturn)
- Copper/Orange (Aquarius/Uranus)
- Aquamarine/Deep Blue (Pisces/Neptune)

Endnotes

[1]The hypersphere is a significant and lasting reflection of our true *angelic* nature. For more in-depth information concerning this interesting fact and for information concerning the human energy field I recommend visiting www.humandesignforusall.com

[2]Dr Karl Jansky was an expert in this particular field of study.

[3]For more information about the intricate dynamics of the hypersphere go to www.sharronrose.com

[4]For more information about the current state of the Earth I recommend *The Joseph Communications* published by *The Band of Light Media.*

The Body's Hypersphere

CHAPTER 3

The Moon's Biorhythms

ACCORDING TO WIKIPEDIA, "THE THEORY of biorhythms claims that one's life is affected by rhythmic biological cycles, and seeks to make predictions regarding these cycles and the personal ease of carrying out tasks related to the cycles. These inherent rhythms are said to control or initiate various biological processes and are classically composed of three cyclic rhythms that are said to govern human behaviour and demonstrate innate periodicity in natural physiological change: the physical, the emotional and the intellectual (or mental) cycles. Others claim there are additional rhythms, some of which may be combinations of the three primary cycles. Some proponents think that biorhythms may be potentially related to bioelectricity and its interactions in the body."

Biorhythm Function

Speaking purely as a proponent, it is my belief that biorhythms, meaning biological rhythms, are connected to the soul and the life force energy; therefore, it would be reasonable to suggest that biorhythms are impulse waves comprised of bioelectrical and electromagnetic energy—infinite energy pulses courtesy of the cosmos. So, by ascertaining the purpose and effects of the biorhythms, we can successfully determine ways to monitor those *ups* and *downs* that frequently occur throughout life—the eternal peregrination.

Taking this viewpoint into consideration, let us now examine the biorhythms in greater detail, and more importantly let us determine their influence from the astrological, medical, and evolutionary perspective.

The theory of biorhythms was discovered in the 1890s by Dr. Wilhem Fliess, a nose and throat specialist; Dr. Hermanna Swoboda, a professor of psychology; and Alfred Telcher, a professor of engineering. Each discovered patterns in the data of recurrent fevers and other illnesses in their patients. The German-born Wilhem Fliess provided the first tentative explanation for this phenomenon on the basis of physiological and emotional cycles.

Biorhythms are often considered by some to be extremely important components in medical astrology because they can indicate the probable cause of an energy drain in a particular chakra or chakras (the higher aspectual rulers of the organs), and once chakras are depleted of energy, the onset of illness or extreme fatigue becomes an almost *inevitable* factor (see Chapter 4, The Chakras).

Ordinarily, there are several ways to calculate the cycles and frequencies of the biorhythms. Long before the advent of computers, basic biorhythm calculations could be achieved with the use of a *biomate* (a German hand held device comprising of three interconnected wheels). The biomate could be operated as soon as the personal details of an individual were entered and once it was rotated the wheels would move in a simultaneous motion thereby displaying the cycles of the biorhythm frequencies. Today there are some very good websites that will equally perform the task in hand.[1]

What Are Biorhythms?

Biorhythms are inherent energy cycles that regulate such things as memory, ambition, coordination, endurance, temperament, and emotion. There are approximately ten biorhythms pulsating throughout the body with each of them having a particular task or function to perform. Interestingly, traditional astrological teachings correlate to the ten planets.

More precisely, biorhythms formulate the body's energy grid; in retrospect they can be easily ascertained as the body's internal energy conduits. From this physiological viewpoint they are easily distinguished as the rudimentary ley lines that galvanize the human anatomy. In addition, biorhythms are interconnected with the chakras in much the same way as the intertwining planetary energies that pulsate throughout the electromagnetic makeup of the cosmos—the synodic cosmic gamut—a diatonic scale of harmonic planetary notes vibrating in different tones and at alternating frequencies. Hypothetically, the Sun could be viewed as an interconnected chakral sphere, and the planets could be seen to symbolise the cosmic *biorhythms*.

Purpose and Function

The purpose and function of the biorhythms is to augment, curtail, and sustain the natural flow of energy throughout the body. The amount of energy that is transmitted to the body at any one time is dependent upon the aspects between the planetary bodies that rule the biorhythms (see further on for more info). In effect the energy that is stored within the biorhythms waxes and wanes and ebbs and flows like the Moon's ecliptic cycles; therefore these random effects of energy losses and gains necessitate our *highs* and *lows* throughout life.

There are three primary biorhythms that support the life force energy: physical, emotional, and intellectual. In addition, there are seven secondary rhythms that support the progression of the soul: spiritual, awareness, aesthetic, intuition, passion, mastery, and wisdom. Each biorhythm is a synchronous representation of the biological clock—an internalized intuitive mechanism. However, unlike the beliefs of some, I cannot subscribe to the notion that the secondary rhythms are combinations of the three primary rhythms; instead it is my belief that biorhythms are separate energy functions performing equally progressive tasks within the human body.

During certain times in our lives the biorhythms can be individually and simultaneously depleted of energy; when simultaneous depletion of the primary rhythms occurs (in other words when all three are low) it is referred to as a "triple critical juncture." Taking a more scientific view, the triple critical juncture is what occurs when all three biorhythms cross the midline—a meridian that separates the active phase from the recovery phase of life (see diagrams later in this chapter).

Alternatively, when a single biorhythm is low it is referred to as a *cautionary* period, and when two or more biorhythms are low it is referred to as a *critical* period. In any case, it is advisable to slow down, rest, and maintain a low profile if and when simultaneous depletion occurs so that full recovery can take place.

This reduced energy loss (whether individual or simultaneous) can be active for up to fourteen days and can orchestrate a maelstrom of confusion within the psyche; the effects can be *multidirectional*, meaning that it can affect many areas of life. This biological dilemma can put the body under immense turmoil and stress.[2] It is believed that the American actress Judy Garland committed suicide at the culmination point of a triple critical junction, thereby indicating severe biorhythm depletion at every level of consciousness (see example later in this chapter).

Planetary Rulers

The planetary rulerships reinforce the Moon's dynamic effect upon the biorhythms. In addition, each biorhythm has an inner planetary as well as an outer planetary ruler. The two secondary rhythms, namely mastery and wisdom, are ruled jointly by the Sun and the social planets: Jupiter and Saturn. These biorhythms with the inclusion of the spiritual biorhythm can be deemed higher support rhythms. In other words, they support the soul's propensity for higher reasoning and expansive learning.

Mastery, for example, reinforces the individual's spirit in its lifelong quest to attain spiritual understanding and achieve mastery of oneself, which is the Sun's intended purpose as taught extensively in the many diverse teachings of astrology. An important point to remember is that the chakras are concerned only with natal planets, whereas the biorhythms are concerned only with transiting planets. This is because chakras, even though they spin, are still *static* points in the body similar to the natal planets in the chart, whereas biorhythms represent continual moving energy vibrations similar to the cosmos.

The Physical Biorhythm

The physical biorhythm completes one life cycle every twenty-three days. This cycle is considered to be the dominant cycle in men. It regulates hand-eye coordination, strength, endurance, sex drive, stamina, initiative, metabolic rate, and resistance to and recovery from illness. Surgery should be avoided on physical transition days and during negative physical cycles. This cycle affects every physical aspect of the human anatomy. It encompasses energy levels, resistance, and overall physical strength and endurance.

Meanwhile, the biorhythm that governs our movements and interactions upon the physical plane is ruled by the inner planet Mars. Mars also rules the secondary biorhythms, aesthetic, and passion. Mars enhances the supple vibrancy of the physical biorhythm through the power of motivation, desire, and impulsiveness. In addition, the physical biorhythm's outer vibration is Pluto, which governs necessary and obligatory transformation on both the physical and evolutionary realms of consciousness. Mars and Pluto are the "alpha and the omega" of the planets. Despite conflicting opinions I have always believed Mars to be the ruler of the LA (Lower Aspects of the psyche), whereas Pluto rules the HA (Higher Aspects). So the physical biorhythm is essential as the vessel that "holds us together."

Difficult aspects between Mars and Pluto will ultimately create enervation and thus fatigue and languidness within the life force energy. Interestingly, at the time of compiling this chapter my own physical biorhythm was moderately *low*, generating an energy output of forty-eight percent efficiency; the culprits were Mars and Pluto, which had made a conjunction in the first house of my birth chart. Traditionally speaking, a conjunction of this calibre would indicate suppressed energy release; however, its effects would be reversed once the physical biorhythm becomes deenergized. Of course there were other planetary factors evident that attributed to my low levels of energy, which included the dampening and weakening influence of Neptune.

Consequently, if the physical biorhythm is undergoing stress the body will be prone to Mars-related disorders such as high blood pressure, glandular fever, muscle dysfunction, and poisoning, especially if Mars and Neptune (intoxicants) are found to be at cross purposes—in opposition for example. During these physical lows, heart attacks and strokes are more likely to occur, especially if the body is experiencing prolonged health problems. In any case this would be a good time to *curtail* physical activities that require a large expenditure of energy.

Venereal disease and other sexually transmitted ailments could also occur at this time, depending in part on the functional efficiency of the secondary biorhythm awareness and the position of Venus and Pluto (a natural polarity) in the chart. Sexually transmitted diseases have in part a powerful lunar catalytic feel about them—an ejaculation of bodily fluids during sexual intercourse is the primary catalyst—and the Moon rules the body's water-based compounds such as proteins and amino acids. Positive aspects between these planets can develop and maximize the potential for awareness, especially the trine, but it needs to be activated because a trine is essentially a *neutral* aspects. Positive aspects can also soften our powers of determination, especially when faced with important and crucial life decisions.

The physical biorhythm with its connection to the sacral chakra is responsible for orchestrating our instinctive need to be multitudinous—to procreate and in many cases to produce several offspring that will keep alive our biological essence, the genes or DNA sequencing that forms a part of the body's chromosomes, which come under the rulership of Pluto. The planets Mars and Pluto are particularly important and helpful when changes need to be implemented upon the life path providing they receive favorable aspects from other planets and signs.

However, when Mars frequents the water sign of Pisces, the individual becomes prone to reccurring energy loss, which often happens on a daily basis, causing listlessness. This energy loss will be personified when the physical biorhythm drops into the recovery zone, causing the native to lose his or her zest for life, or when Mars makes a hard aspect to Saturn or Neptune such as a square. If depression or emotional paralysis (powerlessness) becomes an issue as a result of this energy drain, the native could literally *give up on life*, because life will have somehow lost its appeal or sweetness.

The Emotional Biorhythm

The emotional biorhythm completes one life cycle every twenty-eight days. This cycle is considered to be the dominant one in women. It regulates the emotions, feelings, moods, sensitivity, sensation, sexuality, fantasy, temperament, nerves, reactions, affections, and creativity. This cycle governs the nervous system and is also referred to as the sensitivity rhythm, thereby influencing our emotional states. The emotional biorhythm affects love and hate, optimism and pessimism, passion and coldness, and depression and elation.

The inner planet Venus coordinates its energy patterns with the Moon, thereby increasing or lessening, depending on the nature of the aspect, the biorhythm that rules the body's expression of emotion. The emotional biorhythm's outer planetary vibration is Neptune. In addition, the dwarf planet Vesta also has an influence on this particular biorhythm because it is primarily associated with personal intimacy (unlike Venus at this level). Venus and Neptune also rule the secondary biorhythms of spiritual and intuition. The life cycles of the secondary rhythms are slightly longer than those of the primary rhythms, taking between 38 and 53 days.

Problematic aspects between Venus and Neptune will temporarily drain this biorhythm of energy, causing irritability and emotional blockages such as extreme anxiety and in some cases Moon related illnesses such as IBS (Irritable Bowel Syndrome), especially when squares and inconjunctions are featured. Emotional exhaustion is also likely and even a kind of euphoria is possible; these scenarios occur when an individual experiences highs and lows at the same time, so depression to elation impact simultaneously. Similar to the effects of physical biorhythm depletion, tiredness can also affect emotional lows because exhaustion is often attributed to an imbalanced emotional state.

Positive aspects between these planets operate to a certain degree on an opposing premise, whereby they generate a sense of well-being and instill a feeling of completeness, especially when trines, quintiles, and semi-sextiles are highlighted (semi-sextiles can also be difficult).

During those periods in life when positive aspects are synchronized and working in complete synergy with the emotional biorhythm the ability to express ourselves, especially in relationships, is considerably heightened. It is important to note that the sextile, when working in harmonious synchronization with the emotional biorhythm, operates at its upmost peak efficiency. In other words, it provides an opportunity for joyful and harmonious stimulus, allowing us to connect with our inner sanctum. Emotional biorhythm function is considered to be best suited to the sextile opportunist aspect, providing of course that the opportunity isn't used, for example, to cheat on one's partner.

Traditionally speaking, Venus is revered as the Goddess of Harmony and Wellbeing, and esoterically Neptune is referred to as a *Higher Soulful Consciousness*. When working simultaneously—creating an energy confluence—these cosmic hierarchies determine our instinctive need for emotional lucidity (Neptune), interaction (Venus), and courtship (Vesta). In the progressive sense of the word we also need to be stimulated whereby we can merge or interconnect at the soulful level; this is achieved through the realm of mystic vision, clarity and unconditional love (Neptune).

The emotional biorhythm with its connection to the heart, solar plexus, and root chakra is responsible for providing an inner richness and vitality for life.

The Intellectual Biorhythm

The intellectual biorhythm completes one life cycle every thirty-three days. The intellectual cycle regulates intelligence, logic, mental reaction, alertness and sense of direction, decision-making, judgment, power of deduction, memory, and ambition. It is believed that this particular cycle originates in the brain, thus influencing our ability to learn and reason; it governs the accuracy of computation.

The lunar biorhythm that oversees our cerebral faculties such as our thought processes is ruled by the cosmos's Winged Messenger, Mercury. Mercury stimulates the intellectual biorhythm via the power of rationality and reason, along with its outer planetary vibration, Uranus. In addition both Mercury and Uranus rule the secondary biorhythm of awareness. However, the intellectual biorhythm can often be at odds with the other biorhythms, especially during the difficult transition of a *triple critical junction*. Therefore, the intellectual biorhythm often creates a cathexis, meaning to concentrate mental energy into a single channel of thought, or to become narrow-minded. Narrow-mindedness and rigidity are often early warning signs of this difficult cerebral transition. Ramifications from this crown chakral cathexis can be severe because eventually the mind goes into overload and can see no way out of this intellectual mire of negativity.

Mental breakdowns, psychosis, acute depression, and even suicide are all afflictions contributed to this intellectual trauma that is often the result of the triple critical junction, especially when Mercury and Uranus are found to be at loggerheads, or generally in negative dialogue to other planets. Studies have also revealed that squares, inconjunctions, and especially sesqui-quadrates (an aspect often referred to as the straw that broke the camel's back) between transiting Uranus and Pluto to natal or progressed Mercury are the likely culprits for this inevitable form of mental deterioration.

During periods of mental trauma the intellectual biorhythm can be in conflict with the emotional biorhythm and other secondary biorhythms such as intuition, creating a myriad of negative thoughts and feelings. This continual stream of thought patterns, and especially those troublesome internal dialogues, can often be responsible for the onset of Moon-related indispositions such as ulcers and stomach cramps, and in the worst case scenario tumors can form in the brain or breast cancer can develop as a result of worry and emotional stress.

Positive aspects between Mercury and Uranus can recreate the fundamental disposition toward clarity, unclutteredness, and harmony. Trines especially can rebalance the body's equilibrium, restoring our natural inclination for joy and contentment. Trines between these planets work at maximum efficiency; therefore, a talent for diplomacy and mediation is frequently displayed

The intellectual biorhythm and its association with the crown, third eye, and throat chakra is responsible for providing definition, intelligibility, and distinctive vision. The result is to define and embrace with acceptance and purity the embodiment of life's eternal journey.

Locating Biorhythms in the Birth Chart

Monitoring the biorhythms will assist you in your quest to navigate major astrological transits.

The midline—the line that separates the active and recovery zones—is often considered to be the Ascendant-Descendant polarity. The place where planets are clustered together marks the *active* part of the chart. The areas that are absent of planets are the recovery zones—domains that have been worked on in past lives, indicating that certain aspects of the psyche are in a period of rest and recovery, with the archetypes (signs) assisting this process. More often than not these zones will act as polarity houses for opposing planets and transits so there will still be an element of progression involved with them, but not to the extent that those houses with planets signify. Redundant houses can also signify past life illnesses, and the nature of the illness can be determined via the archetypes of the houses and their ruling planets, which is indicated in the hypersphere.[3]

Just as chakral points are easily located in the birth chart, biorhythms flow at alternating frequencies throughout the chart and can also be easily located; it is simply a matter of being able to determine their location at any given time. Try to imagine or *visualize* the biorhythms as luminescent energy waves pulsating on varying axes and points throughout the birth chart. Ordinarily, they would appear to the viewer as high frequency resonance waves emitting multiple harmonistic tones contrasted by an interconnected vibrancy of color.

Normally, wherever the biorhythm rulerships are aspected marks the flow of a biorhythm through those particular zones of the chart. If, for example, an opposition occurs between transiting Mars and Pluto, or between a transiting planet and a natal planet, the physical biorhythm would flow down the center of the polarity line. The polarity line would then become an intermix of planetary colors. In the case of the square, the biorhythm would flow from one point of contact to the other. The conjunction would simply represent a miniscule point of contact between the planets involved, but the effects would nevertheless be awesome. For biorhythm aspectual interpretation I use orbs no wider than two degrees for the major aspects and one degree for the minor aspects. However, I believe it to be prudent to use these orb calculations in all aspects of astrology, as wide orbs tend to loose their potency and thus their definition.

In the case of the opposition planets, either side of the polarity would also influence the wavelength frequency, especially the apex planet of a t-square. This additional influence would further determine the output and efficiency levels of the biorhythm (for example, it might only be operating at thirty-eight percent efficiency because of the additional influence). If there are more planets on one side of the polarity than the other, the wavelength frequency will be much lower, indicating extreme biorhythm depletion.

These interconnected biorhythms are only affected by the major aspects, i.e. the conjunction, square, and opposition. The minor aspects, namely the sesquiquadrate, inconjunction (aspect of work, health, and adjustment), semi-square, and semi-sextile will orchestrate additional depletion in the biorhythm when they are conjoined with the major aspects. Aside from this they will have little or no effect. Neutral aspects such as trines will also have little or no effect.

Lunar lows (these occur when the transiting Moon makes an opposition to the natal Sun and any planet that occupies the natal Sun sign) can be *classic examples* of biorhythm depletion. However, successfully determining the severity of depletion depends upon other conjoining aspects to the Moon.

This technique can seem complicated but with practice it can be mastered, especially during times when the transiting Sun or the natal Sun receives favorable aspects from other planets, because the Sun rules the biorhythm of mastery.

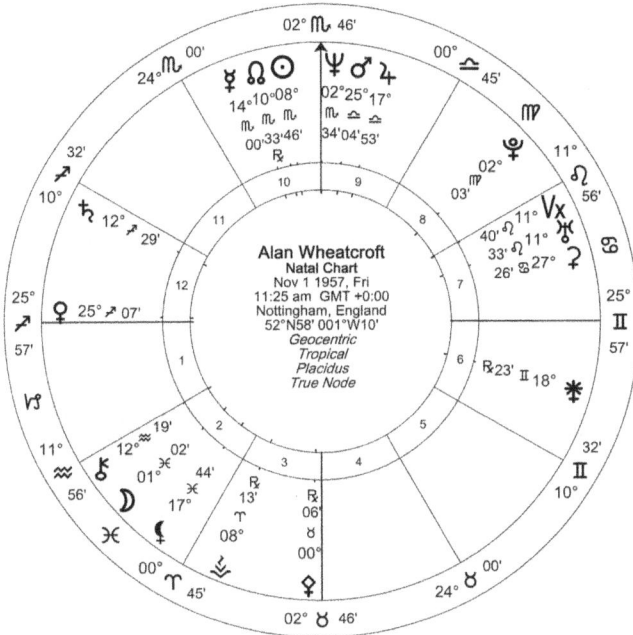

02° ♏ 46'

24° ♏ 00'

☿ ☊ ☉
14°10°08'
♏ ♏ ♏
00'33'46'
℞

♆ ♂ ♃
02°25°17'
♏ ♎ ♎
34'04'53'

10 · 9

00° ♎ 45'

♏

♍ 11°

♇
02°
♍
03'

♌ 56'

Vx
11°
♋ ♌ ♋
40' ♌ 11° ♃
33' ♌ ♋ 27°
26' ♋

32'
10° ♐

♄ 12° ♐ 29'

11

Alan Wheatcroft
Natal Chart
Nov 1 1957, Fri
11:25 am GMT +0:00
Nottingham, England
52°N58' 001°W10'
Geocentric
Tropical
Placidus
True Node

8

7

25°
♐ 57'

♀ 25° ♐ 07'

12

25°
♊ 57'

♋ 25°

♊ 25°

♋

℞23' ♊ 18' ✳

6

♊ 10° 32'

♓ 11° ♒ 56'

⚸ 01° ♒ 44'

☽ 17° ♓

♒ 12° ♓ 02'

19'

2

℞ 13' ♈ 08°

3

4

℞ 06' ♉ 00°

5

24° ♉ 00'

00° ♈ 45'

⚷

♀

02° ♉ 46'

Personal Case Study

During a critical triple juncture in my life, on November 26, 2012, a conjunction occurred between Mars and Pluto in Capricorn in my first house. Mars and Pluto indicated that physical biorhythm depletion was inevitable. The strength of the depletion was determined by Capricorn, which indicated that my left brain functions were low and that I would have difficulty concentrating and focusing on practical matters during this period. The first house indicated that depletion would occur in my head. In addition, every one of my secondary rhythms, with the exception of intuition and self-awareness, was in the recovery zone at the time.

Furthermore, Venus and Saturn in Scorpio had made a conjunction in my tenth house, indicating further soul depletion in my emotional, spiritual, and intuition biorhythms. Mercury's

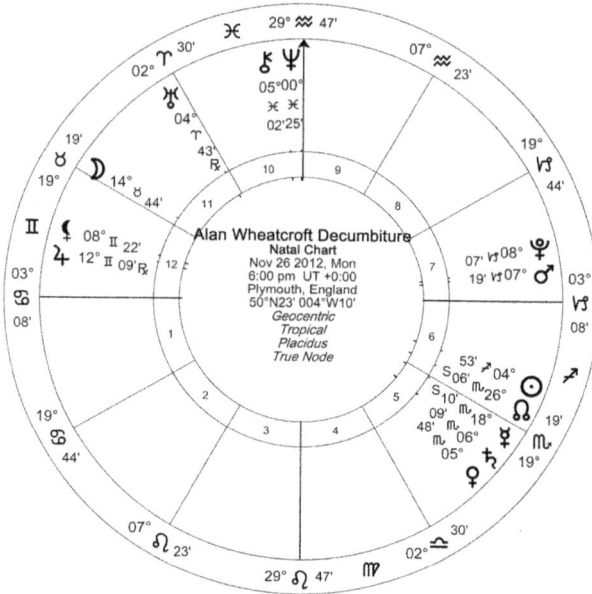

Alan R. Wheatcroft

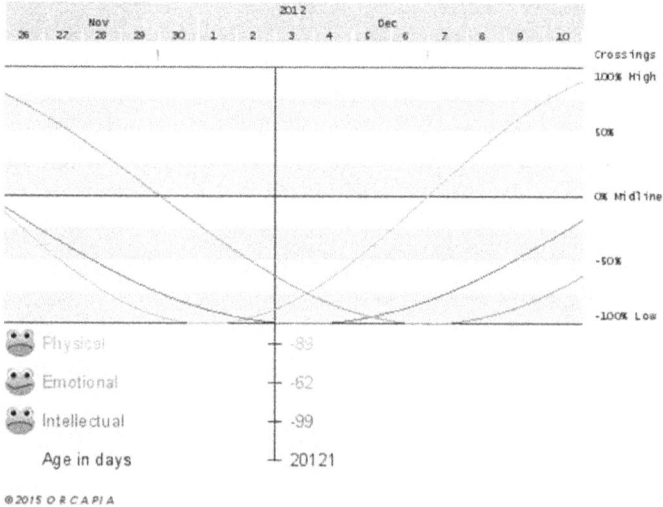

		2012				
Nov				Dec		

Crossings
100% High

50%

0% Midline

-50%

-100% Low

😠 Physical   ─ -89

😠 Emotional   ─ -62

😠 Intellectual   ─ -99

Age in days   ─ 20121

Figure 1: Primary Rhythm

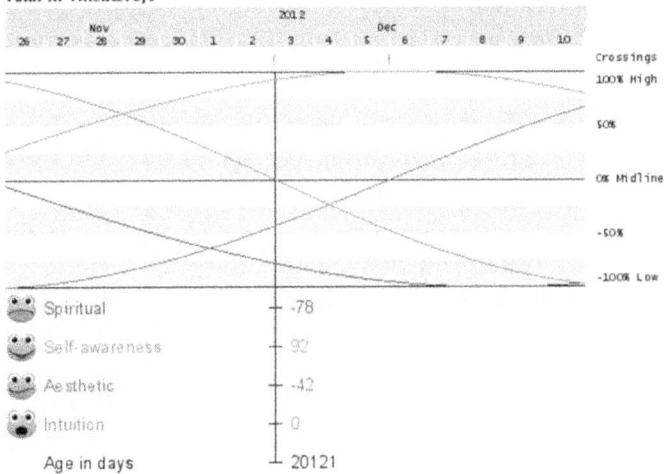

Alan R. Wheatcroft

Spiritual	-78	
Self-awareness	92	
Aesthetic	-42	
Intuition	0	
Age in days	20121	

Figure 2: Secondary Rhythms

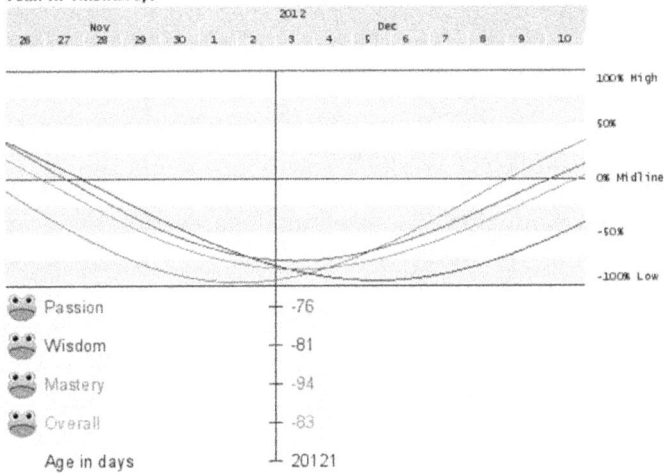

Alan R. Wheatcroft

Passion	-76	
Wisdom	-81	
Mastery	-94	
Overall	-83	
Age in days	20121	

Figure 3: Secondary Rhythms

One Body Many Illnesses   39

retrograde cycle, also in Scorpio, was the primary significator for intellectual biorhythm depletion. At the very beginning of the depletion Mercury received an opposition from the Moon and a sesquiquadrate from Uranus.

Uranus was the apex planet that linked it to all of these bio aspects, indicating sudden, unpredictable, and chaotic disharmony in my higher mind functions (see charts and biorhythms on the following pages). For the first time in many years I felt a sense of overwhelming discord and furthermore my normally unwavering spiritual faith had somehow abandoned me—a disturbing prospect in a world of uncertainty.

Finally, it is important to note that during the influence of major transits, especially when they involve the outer planets, biorhythm depletion will be unusually *high* during the transition, meaning that the ebbs and flows will become more erratic and frequent than usual.

Judy Garland

Judy Garland's body was discovered at 10:50 am on June 22, 1969, in London. She had ingested an overdose of sleeping pills, a habit she reportedly began at an early age. A potential addiction to these types of drugs is indicated by Neptune's tight inconjunction to Uranus with the Sun's mutable t-square between retrograde Mars and Uranus intercepting it. As Neptune (emotional biorhythm) rules the mind's unconscious state—the dream world—an aspect such as this, especially when linked with Uranus the awakener, would have been tantamount to a division opening within the psyche that orchestrated deep emotional turmoil and endless brain activity. Notably, this would have led to the onset of severe sleep deprivation. Essentially, her body would not have been able to correctly interpret the brain's convoluted message, whereby it was attempting to point out that is was time to sleep.

The Sun-Mars opposition (physical and mastery biorhythm)

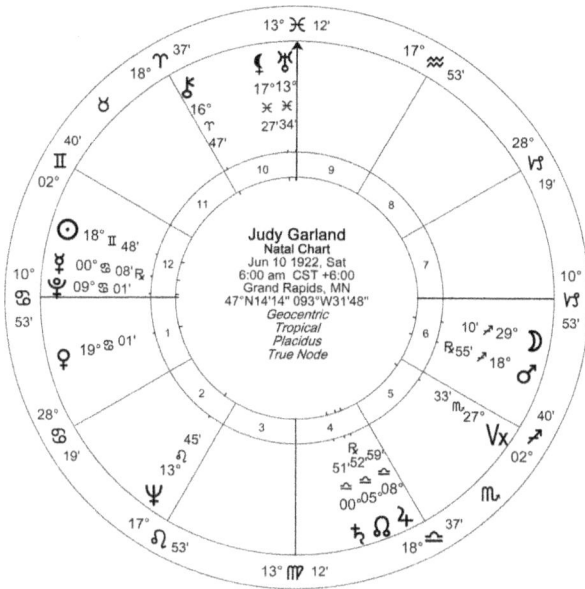

Judy Garland
Natal Chart
Jun 10 1922, Sat
6:00 am CST +6:00
Grand Rapids, MN
47°N14'14" 093°W31'48"
Geocentric
Tropical
Placidus
True Node

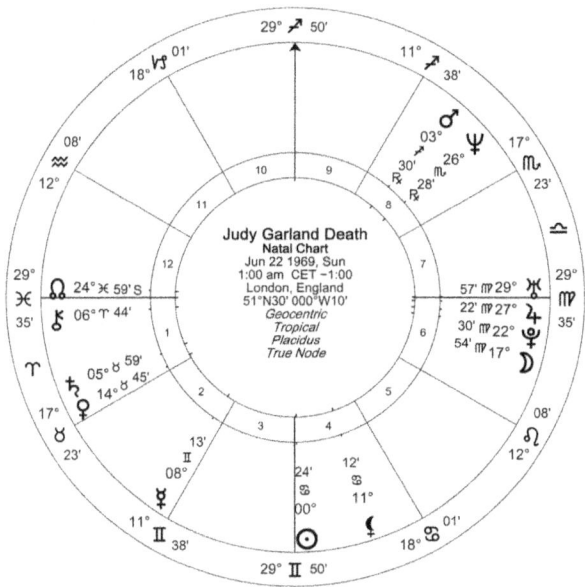

Judy Garland Death
Natal Chart
Jun 22 1969, Sun
1:00 am CET −1:00
London, England
51°N30' 000°W10'
Geocentric
Tropical
Placidus
True Node

One Body Many Illnesses

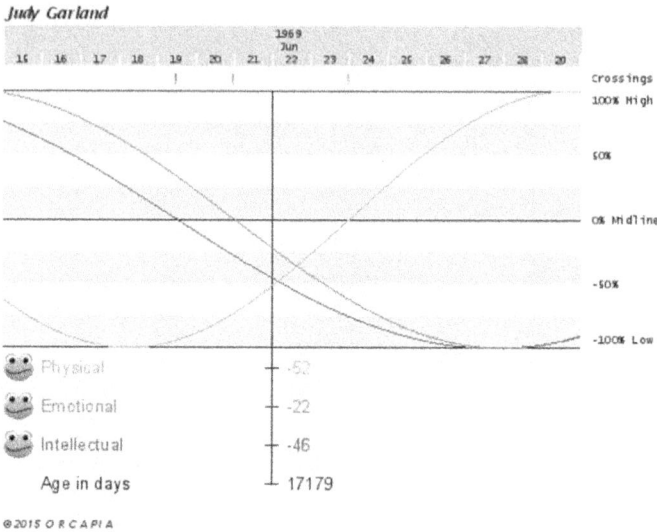

Judy Garland

| | | | | | 1969 Jun | | | | | | | |
|16|16|17|18|19|20|21|22|23|24|25|26|27|28|20|

Crossings
100% High
50%
0% Midline
-50%
-100% Low

😊 Physical | -52
😊 Emotional | -22
😊 Intellectual | -46
Age in days | 17179

©2015 ORCAPIA

Figure 1: Primary Rhythms

in the twelfth-sixth house polarity would also have been a contributing factor to sleep deprivation along with retrograde Mercury's (intellectual and wisdom biorhythm) square to Saturn. Both these aspects would have denoted severe anxiety with the potential occurrence of panic attacks. Because of mind chatter and cerebral overload Judy would not have mastered the ability to achieve a proper and peaceful night's sleep. Clearly she would have suffered many sleepless nights as a result of these powerful bio-afflictions. Because of the profound influence of Uranus, her increasing addiction to drugs would quite likely have been the result of a sudden inclination to ingest more, hence a higher dosage. Interestingly, the coroner indicated that death most likely occurred around 1:00 am. Assuming he was correct, it provides an ample basis to delineate the death chart.

Although there are a multitude of contributing factors indicating the cause of death, the triple critical junction of biorhythm depletion is highlighted by the mutable grand cross configura-

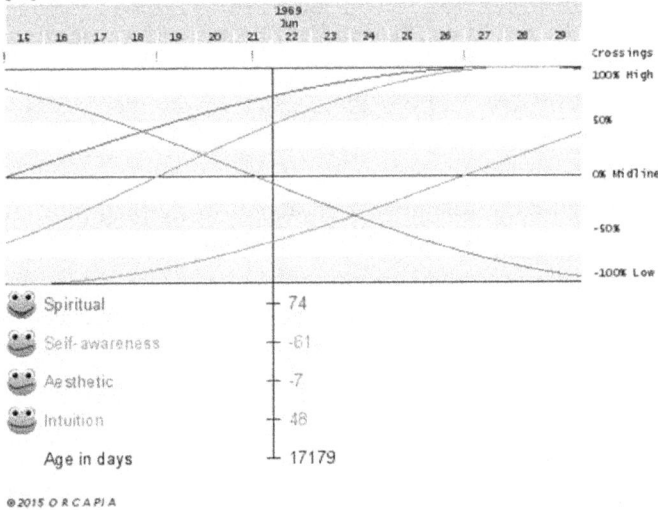

Judy Garland

1969
Jun

| 15 | 16 | 17 | 18 | 19 | 20 | 21 | 22 | 23 | 24 | 25 | 26 | 27 | 28 | 29 |

Crossings
100% High
50%
0% Midline
-50%
-100% Low

😊 Spiritual — 74
😠 Self-awareness — -61
😊 Aesthetic — -7
😐 Intuition — 48

Age in days — 17179

© 2015 O R C A P I A

Figure 2: Secondary Rhythms

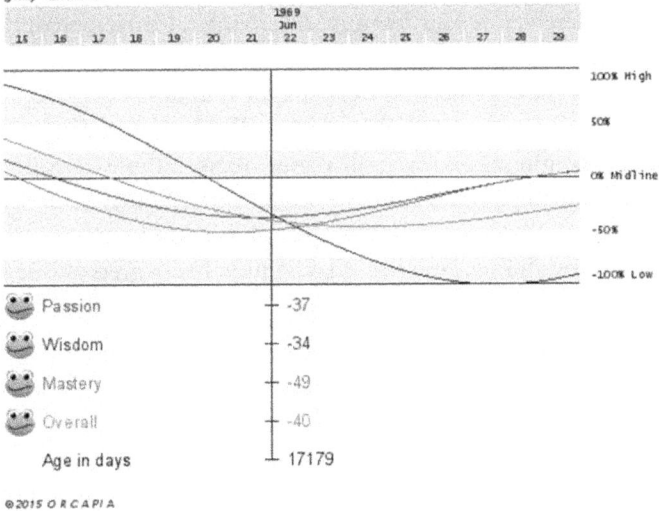

Judy Garland

1969
Jun

| 15 | 16 | 17 | 18 | 19 | 20 | 21 | 22 | 23 | 24 | 25 | 26 | 27 | 28 | 29 |

100% High
50%
0% Midline
-50%
-100% Low

😊 Passion — -37
😊 Wisdom — -34
😊 Mastery — -49
😐 Overall — -40

Age in days — 17179

© 2015 O R C A P I A

Figure 3: Secondary Rhythms

One Body Many Illnesses   43

tion between the Ascendant in Pisces, Sun in Gemini, Uranus in Virgo, and the Midheaven in Sagittarius. Ordinarily this effect would cause mental conflict and confusion within the psyche; however, the mutable effect of this partly angular grand cross receiving hard aspects from Pluto could be another indication of the deep-set inner turmoil she had endured throughout life, maybe towards her employers. It is believed that her employers were partly responsible for her addiction to sleeping pills. This would seem likely as the death chart brings this to light with the Neptune-ruled Node opposing the quadrature of planets in work-orientated Virgo. The Neptune and Node interception of the Ascendant also vindicate this hypothesis as these significators would orchestrate further self-judgment and criticism.

Mercury's opposition to retrograde Mars signifies a conflict between the intellectual, physical, awareness, and aesthetic biorhythms. Furthermore, Mars's malefic conjunction to Neptune from eighth house of death and tragedy signifies a conflict between the physical, spiritual, and emotional biorhythms (see chart and figure 1). This is further vindicated by the sesquiquadrate between Venus and Uranus, signifying an extreme conflict between the emotional and intellectual biorhythms. Note also that the physical biorhythm overlaps the emotional and intellectual biorhythms in the recovery zone. The Moon's conjunction to Pluto would instill fear and regret because the Moon is the ruler of her birth chart and the ruler of the biorhythms. This powerful configuration would signify childhood frustration that carried through into later life. Maybe Judy had regrets about the way she cared for her own children.

It is said that when biorhythms overlap each other the effects can create extreme mental turmoil and confusion within the psyche. Figures 2 and 3 also indicate secondary biorhythm depletion with the similar overlapping effect, but with the exception of the spiritual and intuition rhythms. In effect this triple critical junction of biorhythm depletion was activated by the eighth house of death with Neptune's connection to social and prescription drugs. Neptune's rulership of the twelfth house and the North Node, with its inevitable connection to the Creator, meant that it was time to go and for her to meet her *maker*.

Conclusion

This chapter has established that the Moon's biorhythms play an important and effective role in the birth chart. When planets transit the birth chart and form difficult aspects it is time to check those biorhythms. Interestingly, biorhythm depletion is most likely responsible for difficult and traumatic births and birth defects. Biorhythm depletion at birth is of course a representation of those planetary alignments starting to inflict their influence, some of which can obfuscate the transition onto the physical plane.

Endnotes

[1]Website recommendation, www.biorhythms.com/raid

[2]The psychoanalyst Carl Jung believed in the importance and composite effects of the biorhythms especially upon the body during periods of *triple critical junctions*.

[3]For an in-depth analysis on past life patterns and undertakings I recommend reading *Understanding Karmic Complexes* by Patricia L. Walsh, published by The Wessex Astrologer.

CHAPTER 4

The Solar Chakras

*"The only way we can attain true fulfilment and joy in
this life is when we listen to the evolutionary calling of the
soul. Once we resonate with its divine harmonic frequency
this infinite source of energy becomes our guide upon the
eternal journey of life."*—Kabir, mystic philosopher

CHAKRAS (THE ORGANS OF THE soul) are the storehouses and
transmitters of the soul energy. They are multi-colored energy
vortices located in different positions along the spinal column.

In Sanskrit the chakras represent the *Antahkarana* or *Rainbow Bridge*, which is a term also used in Vedic astrology, the
rainbow bridge signifying the traditional colors of the rainbow
and the interconnection between the Lower and Higher Aspects
of the psyche. In one of her earliest publications the astrologer
Barbara Hand Clow used the rainbow bridge analogy to effectively describe Chiron. Throughout the last 2,500 years or so,
there have always been seven chakras, although some esoteric
teachings have determined that there are in fact eight, the eighth
being located at the very tip of the crown.

From the root to the crown the colors of the chakras are identified in the following sequence: red, orange, yellow, green, blue,
indigo, and violet, with the possible eighth chakra being translucent. Incidentally, rainbows are Earth's way of reflecting its
chakras. Chakras are also the reason why human beings vibrate a

low-resonance energy field we frequently refer to as the *aura*. Primarily speaking, chakras represent the energy of the Sun that is prevalent in every soul that frequents the Earth-plane. However, the strength and purpose of this energy is dependent on the Sun sign and its respective aspects. However, with Leo and the other fire signs the chakras retain a high energy yield.

Below is a list of the traditional chakras and their rulership signs:

- **Root chakra**: co-ruled by Taurus/Capricorn
- **Sacral chakra**: co-ruled by Aries/Scorpio
- **Solar plexus**: ruled by Virgo
- **Heart chakra**: co-ruled by Leo
- **Throat chakra**: co-ruled by Gemini/Sagittarius
- **Third eye**: co-ruled by Cancer/Pisces
- **Crown chakra**: co-ruled by Libra/Aquarius

Chakral Purpose

Chakras play a crucial role in helping to maintain the body's internal organs and they also assist in helping to balance the energy of the soul. Chakras help us to understand the soul's dialogue at the higher spiritual level, meaning that they act as messengers carrying messages from the Higher Aspects of the psyche.

Spiritual Transformation

Throughout this time of great uncertainty and change upon Earth, and particularly since the end of 2011, the chakras are helping to orchestrate the supple but profound personal changes that many people have began undertaking. These changes are in line with those that are occurring on the Earth.[1] Essentially the chakras are helping us to achieve the universal process of TSI (Total Soul Integration), occurring from 2012 to the end of

2015, beginning the second decanate of the Aquarian Age—the Age of Reform. Most notably is that the Age of Aquarius is now in full flow so to speak and has been since the beginning of the industrial revolution. But unfortunately there is much controversy about this.

The Chakras of the Aquarian Age

As we, the human collective consciousness, transcend further into the Aquarian Age, the energy of each chakra will begin resonating at a higher base frequency, increasing its geometric field and influence. This proliferative transformation will significantly alter the dynamics and appearance of the chakras and create a universal juxtaposition in human consciousness.

As a result of this shift, colors will change, manifesting an entirely new spectrum. This transcendence in color coordination has already begun—a transformation that began at the start of the new millennium. No longer will the chakras be comprised of *single colors*. Instead, they will be infused with the colours of the planetary rulers of the Aquarian Age: Jupiter, Saturn, and Uranus—an astrological stellium that represents both the *exoteric* and *esoteric* rulerships.

The new colors are violet (Jupiter), petrol blue (Saturn), and petrol green (Uranus). Also, the new-look chakras will be imbued with the metallic compounds of gold (Jupiter), silver (Saturn), and copper (Uranus/Chiron), representing the Higher Aspects of the psyche. Copper is formed by an intermix process of the other two elements. The merging of the higher elements into a single force is essentially what Uranus represents. The new style chakras are thus an intermixed combination of these colors.

In addition this results in a significant shift in their overall composition and size, meaning that the individual dimensions of each chakra intensify. Five additional chakras of the HA (Higher Aspects) will be integrated into the psyche, making twelve in total during the first sub-decanate (50 years) of the Age of Reform.

The purpose of the five additional chakras is to interface with the higher brain functions. Once the new chakras have been successfully integrated we will possess the ability to connect with the higher octave vibrations of telepathy, psychic healing, telekinesis and clairaudience.[2]

The five additional chakras and their rulership signs, which are the co-rulers of the traditional chakras, are:

- HA1: the chakra of the soul configuration, ruled by Scorpio.
- HA2: the chakra of the right brain ascension, ruled by Sagittarius.
- HA3: the chakra of the left brain ascension, ruled by Capricorn.
- HA4: the chakra of the higher-mind configuration, ruled by Aquarius.
- HA5: the chakra of the divine Creationery Source, ruled by Pisces.[3]

Chakral Transformation

At night when we close our eyes and go to sleep, and also in our dreams, we begin to see colors forming in the third eye chakra; these are the colors that emanate from the other chakras. The colors we see most clearly are the ones that are representative of the aspected planets in our natal chart. For example, if the Moon is in Pisces opposing Pluto in Virgo we would see the deep blue of Pisces contrasted by the deep yellow hue of Virgo.

However, the overall view seems to be that people more often see the color violet; coupled with much deeper shades of blue and green, the colour violet purports the healing potential of the violet flame. This is evidence that the chakras *have* and *are* indeed being *surpassed*.

Chakral Colorations

Since the start of the new millennium the chakras have undertaken a process of transformation. The new changes are as follows: The root chakra becomes a copper gold vortex into which, as it spins, ribbons of energy appear made up of strips of clear gold, violet and petrol blue. The sacral chakra becomes a clear petrol blue with ribbons of clear gold, violet and copper gold. The solar plexus becomes a clear petrol green with ribbons of clear gold, violet and petrol blue. The heart chakra changes to a transparent energy shimmering with ribbons and flecks of all the other colors. The throat chakra becomes transparent with random flecks of all the other colors covering the whole surface. The third eye becomes transparent with random flecks of all the other colors, but with less than the fifth. And finally the crown chakra becomes totally transparent without any flecks, just pure energy. By visualizing and working with the new colors healers and practitioners will be empowered with the energies of the new age.

Now that I have provided a brief insight into the dynamics of the chakras let us begin a further analysis by examining the conditions that can arise in a physical capacity when a chakra orchestrates bodily malfunction and breakdown. We begin with an analysis of the seventh chakra, know otherwise as the root or base, and finish with an analysis of the first chakra, hence the crown.

The Root Chakra

This chakra is located at the base of the spine and at the tip of the coccyx. Consequently, it is affected if we start feeling *insecure* about life and especially if our levels of self-confidence begin to wane. The root chakra relates to the skeleton, muscles, and skin in general and to the urinary system. So if we begin feeling somewhat insecure, especially in daily life or in specific situations, the skin is affected and eczema or dermatitis can develop. If, however, we refuse to alter our situation, the muscles will begin aching or *complaining*, and if we continue to ignore our insecurities and these early warning symptoms the bones can become infected similar to the conditions of osteoporosis. Interestingly, osteoporosis has nothing to do with hormones—just long term insecurity.

The urinary system can also become affected if there is a situation we have been trying to deal with remains ongoing. Insecurities of this kind are related to incontinence in the elderly.

The Sacral Chakra

This chakra is located where the spine meets the pelvis, at the top of the sacrum bone. The sacral chakra relates to the sexual reproduction organs, the testes, and the prostate in men and the uterus and ovaries in women.

The majority of problems that arise with these organs are when we start having difficulties with our partners. However, if we learn to understand the primary role of this chakra, which is about interconnection and embracing our creativity, and hence rediscover our creative side, partnership issues can be overcome.

In addition, if we have "structural problems" in the sacral region such as lower back, pelvic, or hip pain, it is because we feel *insecure* within our sexual relationships or within our creativity. To achieve *sexual* contentment the sacral chakra needs to be satisfied and cleansed via the interaction of deep and spiritually-rewarding bonding or physical intercourse.

The Solar Plexus

This chakra is located in the middle spine more or less in line with the tummy button. The main concern of the solar plexus is with personal power issues. In addition it has a secondary function by which it is connected to the emotions we express or don't express. The organs related to this chakra are: the liver, gall bladder, pancreas, spleen, stomach, and intestines.

Essentially the liver is the central processor for every kind of emotion that manifests in the body. More importantly, the liver distributes them to the appropriate organs; for example, the gall bladder deals with unexpressed anger. The liver, however, deals with the emotions of guilt, jealousy, and fear. The pancreas relates to the suppressed energy that we should display when expressing ourselves; for example, if we feel we should have shouted in a situation but instead only muttered under our breath, then all that unexpressed emotion affects the pancreas.

The spleen deals with frustration, especially frustration connected with unexpressed anger. Another function of the spleen is to oversee the lower lymphatic system. So if we store up too much anger and frustration, the lymphatic begins to block up with cellulite and lower body weight gain. The stomach deals with short-term emotional storage and the large intestine deals with long-term emotional storage. The small intestine is a processor for emotional storage.

The Heart Chakra

This chakra is located at roughly the same point as the physical heart. Aside from protecting the heart, it deals with the blood circulation and the upper lymphatic system. It also deals with the thymus gland and the endocrine system—the body's hormone system.

Essentially, the heart chakra acts as the center of communication between the soul and the physical body—hence the term "spiritual heart." In effect the soul uses the body's hormones to communicate to the higher mind that we have somehow lost our sense of direction and *strayed* from the soul's chosen path. Another function of the heart chakra is the expression of love, either for the self or others.

Heart problems and conditions, which are all related to this chakra, usually have to do with our expression of love. So for example, if we are not good at expressing our love to those who are closest to us or to humanity itself, the physical heart will eventually be affected. If, on the other hand, we are not particularly good at expressing love to ourselves (and not in the narcissistic sense of the word) the thymus and upper lymphatic system becomes blocked. Interestingly, women are not generally good at this form of self-expression; therefore, the ultimate outcome of denial at this level is breast cancer. When men don't express themselves the wall of the heart or the arteries have a tendency to harden.

The Throat Chakra

This chakra is located in the throat, just above the Adam's apple. At its primary level the main function of the throat chakra is that of self-expression, and communication and judgment at its secondary level. The connecting organs are the lungs and the thyroid.

The lungs represent expression, while the thyroid represents how comfortable we feel in expressing ourselves. Lung diseases such as tuberculosis, alveolitis, pulmonary fibrosis, emphysema and sarcoidosis, and even asthma are all diseases connected to suppressed expression and stagnant or stifled creativity.

The thyroid also controls the body's levels of calcium, particularly in the spinal chord. In addition, the thyroid controls the body's metabolism—how effectively we use oxygen within the body to metabolize our food. A slow and *underactive* thyroid relates to an individual who needs to feel important or who wants to look bigger than he or she actually feels inside. An *overactive* thyroid, however, relates to someone who loses weight in hopes of disappearing into the background, unnoticed. Communication is a very important component in the life plan!

The Third Eye Chakra

This chakra is located in the center of the forehead, just above the bridge of the nose. Its primary function represents the part of our consciousness that deals with our spirituality, our sense of soul. The chakra has a secondary function: our psychic vision. Blockages occur in this chakra when we refuse to acknowledge and thus disengage ourselves from our spiritual purpose. Furthermore, the third eye chakra is connected to our primary senses: the nose, as in the need for smell; the ears, as in the need to hear; the left eye, as in the need to see; and the lower brain and the central nervous system, as in the need to sense. Respiratory complaints, labyrinthitis, deafness and blindness are all consequences of this chakra when it begins to malfunction.

The third eye chakra also oversees the pituitary gland, which is the controlling gland for the endocrine system: the soul's messengers. But do we want to listen to the soul?

The Crown Chakra

This chakra is located at the very top of the head in a direct line with the spinal column. The point of the chakra's vortex is connected to the top of the head therefore the vortex opens directly upwards. More important, the crown chakra is our *direct* energetic connection to the non-physical aspects of the psyche such the higher self.

The crown chakra represents the upper part of the brain, our thoughts, and our center of wisdom. It also represents the right eye and through the right eye it connects to the pineal gland, the gland situated at the base of the brain that produces the hormone called melatonin.

Melatonin works with our psychic functions; however, Chronic Fatigue Syndrome is also a consequence manufactured by this particular hormone. If we have have removed ourselves so far from the guidance of the soul and refuse to listen to any of its promptings, the crown chakra initiates production of melatonin; then all we can do is slow down until we sort out the mess we have inadvertently made for ourselves.

Although this is the briefest of guides about the chakras, it provides insight into how the chakras are responsible for the onset of illness. The chakras do communicate with us, but as with many things in life, we have forgotten how to listen. More information about the chakras can be attained in my book, *Evolution and the Cosmic Clock*.

From a chakral point of view, let us now examine the birth chart of actor Patrick Swayze, who died a few years ago of pancreatic cancer.

Patrick Swayze

Patrick was born with a fixed Grand Cross, which in my opinion was the primary catalyst for the onset of this terminal disease. Patrick's North Node, representing the current life path, is in Aquarius, and when the North Node transits this air sign it signifies oxidization, meaning a continual loss of oxygen from the body's cells. This affliction is also emphasised when the North Node is in hard aspect to the luminaries, Saturn, or Neptune, and in Patrick's case the North Node is opposing his Sun in the twelfth house. The North Node is also in oblique opposition to the Leo stellium of Mercury, Pluto, and the South Node, which all resonate as an echo from a past life or lives.

In addition we should consider the position of the South Node as being partially *besieged*, meaning it has been blockaded by planetary forces and furthermore it is being *harassed* by these planetary forces. Translated, this means: the likelihood of unfinished business is evident in the chart, especially as Pluto (the planet of death and the pancreas) is also besieged. This powerful configuration would also indicate that the cosmic signature embedded into any potential illness would most definitely be karmic. This notion is further vindicated by Venus's occupation of the twelfth house of karma and past life associations and connections, and with Venus ruling the eighth house of death.

Uranus as accidental ruler of the fifth house signifies a polar-

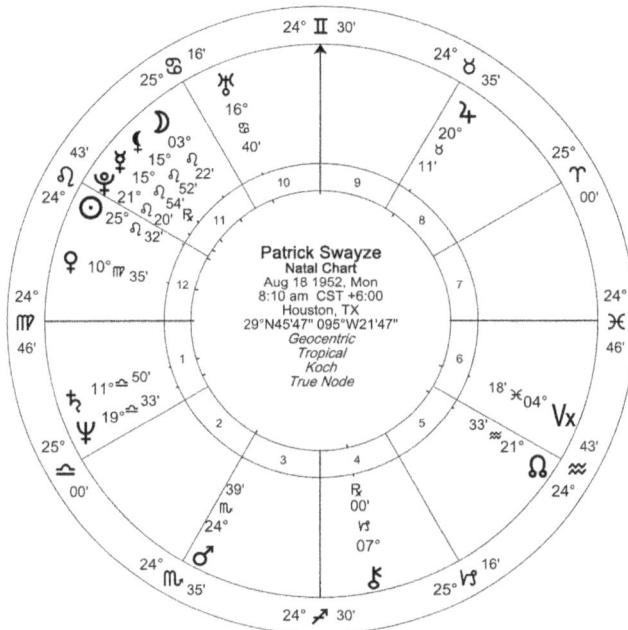

ized shift in chakral energies, meaning that the chakras representing the heart and higher mind could have become unexpectedly *imbalanced*. In addition, the fifth house would represent the home for his Higher Aspects. In retrospect, Patrick's pancreatic cancer was triggered by a combination of unpredictable and negative energies that essentially overwhelmed his heart's immune system (Leo), creating a severe imbalance of chakral energy along the Solar-Nodal polarity that emanated from the fifth house. In essence, his "sweetness for life" (pancreas) had somehow dissipated.

When Aries is at zero degrees, Leo becomes the natural ruler of the fifth house quadrant; therefore, it comes as no surprise that Patrick decided to begin a career in acting, indicated in part by his Leo Sun in opposition to his North Node. Saturn's position from the first house also ruling the fifth means that it is quite likely he became a workaholic. Saturn's semi-sextile to Venus and Neptune's sextile to Pluto suggests that *overwork* weakened his immune system with Pluto ruling the second house of constitution. I am always very aware of sextiles and semi-sextiles because in the worst-case scenario these aspects can be *poisonous*.

Patrick was considered a nice guy throughout the acting profession; however, I suspect that he suppressed many of his opinions. His suppressed opinions were most likely to have been the result of planets in the twelfth house with Mercury conjoining the South Node and opposing the North Node. Suppressed opinions may also be the result of inner tension and conflict, which is denoted by his Sun-South Node conjunction—perhaps incoherencies from past lives. Mercury's wide-arc conjunction to Jupiter could also indicate some unresolved mental issues and a conflict of ideals as Jupiter is square the Nodes. Inner conflict is a further indication for the onset of illness because it quells the sweetness for life symbolized by the pancreas.

According to Alan Oken the Moon is the esoteric ruler of Virgo, which is also connected to the pancreas, and the Moon is associated with fluid retention. In this case pancreatic cancer would slow down the natural function of the digestive system (the solar plexus), thus disrupting the flow of pancreatic fluids to the gut. Pluto signifies cell mutation, and thus the bombardment of cancerous cells to the pancreas and upper lymphatic system would have been brought about by chakral depletion to the solar plexus and heart chakra. Pluto's oblique opposition to the North Node and its conjunction to the South Node would surely indicate the onset of free radicals in extreme overload.

Pancreatitis

Pancreatic cancer is often triggered when the individual has been subjected to long-term chronic pancreatitis. Chronic and acute pancreatitis occur when calcium deposits (gall stones) become trapped in the pancreatic and bile ducts, causing inflammation of the pancreas. Over time, scarring to the pancreas is likely and inevitably causes severe damage to this important organ. As pancreatic function falls under the rulership of Pluto it is absolutely crucial that balance is maintained in the solar plexus at all times; otherwise Pluto can severely affect the body's metabolism via this organ. The most common and *prolific* aggravant to trigger the onset of pancreatitis is alcohol. Frequently I have seen this condition diagnosed in the horoscopes of people where Saturn and Pluto afflict the Moon, Venus, or Neptune, or a combination of those factors.

It seems likely that at some point Patrick would have suffered from chronic pancreatitis, a condition indicative of Venus's affliction (semi-sextile) to Saturn. Neptune's inconjunction to Jupiter and its square to Uranus in Cancer would also have been important significators of this disease. These aspects would have orchestrated problems in the abdominal region of the body signified by Venus's transit of Virgo (solar plexus). What is not clear is whether Patrick developed an alcohol addiction; however, Neptune's inconjunction to Jupiter and square to Uranus would seem to indicate that alcohol reliance may have been evident at some stage throughout his life.

Death

Death, or *rebirth* as I prefer to call it, is the fundamental and inevitable conclusion to physical incarnation. Unfortunately, it is still an issue that many fear and even disregard, mainly because of the kind of death that could ensue. In Patrick's case the cause of his death was highlighted by Mars's oblique opposition to Jupiter, and in many cases Jupiter represents the final journey. As Mars and Jupiter are key players in the Grand Cross, death from pancreatic cancer would have been a certainty, and furthermore it would not have been a swift transition. Mars opposes the fixed star Algol and Venus is at the midpoint, so it would be reasonable to assume that it was a painful and stressful transition.

Interestingly, Neptune's inconjunction to Jupiter extemporized that a period of recovery, and in Patrick's case a point of remission, would occur, bringing reconciliation and diversion from the annals of this wasting disease. Note that both planets are in Venus-ruled signs and that the inconjunction is an aspect that symbolizes *adjustment* and *recovery*. Patrick was diagnosed with this condition in January 2008 and did not die until September 2009, indicating that the cancer went into remission (September is a Virgo month and represents the solar plexus).

But because of Neptune's transit of Libra from the first house of physicality, which represented his crown chakra, his will and energy eventually weakened (Neptune); he gave up the fight and the will to live, thus surrendering to this illness. Also, the Nodes were clearly a source of *trauma* and *tragedy* in Patrick's life, which was linked to the fact that the South Node was besieged and the North Node was opposing the Leo stellium.

Final Analysis

Overall the pattern that formed in Patrick's chart was one that indicated a complete chakral imbalance. Clearly the pancreatic cancer was a disposition of his previous incarnations—perhaps something he failed to achieve—causing subconscious discord and anger and symbolized in part by Pluto's exact conjunction to the South Node. This deep-set and prolific anger was often evident in his remarkable films, especially *Ghost*, which manifested via his Sun-North Node opposition. Working with the chakras can help to determine the root cause of every type of illness and therefore outline the best possible chance for prognosis and recovery.

Endnotes

[1] For more information about personal and global change I would suggest referring to the combined works of *Zecharia Sitchin*.

[2] Information courtesy of the Akashic Records. The Akashic is also the source of the chakral interpretations.

[3] Further information courtesy of the Akashic Records.

Part 2

Nodal Interpretation

CHAPTER 5

The Moon's South Node: Conciliation

"The lunar Nodes are heavenly cosmic projections
hence celestial symbols that communicate with the part of
the psyche that knows our destiny."—Alan R. Wheatcroft

THE NEXT TWO CHAPTERS EXAMINE the Nodes merely from an evolutionary perspective, which, to a degree, explains why the Nodes are extremely important factors throughout the practice of medical astrology. Illness and disease, whether manifesting as a singular affliction or as an interconnected combination, are representative to the concepts of trauma and tragedy, to which the Nodes are associated. The diverse principles of *trauma* and *tragedy* and their association with the Nodes are examined in greater detail further on.

Evolutionary astrology (meaning Pluto centered) determines that Pluto and its polarity point to the evolutionary progression of the soul. Moreover, the evolutionary progression of the soul is also symbolized by the Moon's North and South Node. Popular consensus indicates that the North Node signifies futuristic potential and soul growth, but its nascent vibrations remain *unnerving* and sometimes *unfamiliar* until we begin to learn that evolutionary transformation is an important and necessary facet of our soul. Whereas the Moon's South Node is said to be an evolutionary representation of the soul's experiences throughout a past incarnation/incarnations, the South Node is equated to a cosmic compendium of past-life expressions and experiences that were once symbolized by the cyclic polarity point of the North Node.

In retrospect the energy of the South Node is reinforced when the North Node potential is not realized or facilitated. In order to achieve maximum potential from the Nodal polarity the energy of the Nodes must therefore be filtered and integrated, and special attention must be paid to the clarion call of the North Node. Ordinarily the Nodes should be given similar credence to that which is placed upon the fundamental principle of chart polarities—that the energy of a planet is directed toward the polarity to which it manifests. Polarities define the term "opposites attract."

The South Node: the Familiar Calling

Before I begin my analysis I point out that the South Node is in *exaltation* in Sagittarius and is in its *fall* in Gemini. This is an important factor to consider because any personalized karma (meaning trauma and tragedy) is often emphasized via these lunar archetypes. When the Nodes are in dignity and detriment, and depending on associated planetary aspects, mental health issues can often become a pervading force that can manifest when transiting planets are rendered *unfavorable*. Through all of my many case studies this seems to be a common occurrence with those individuals who had this particular Nodal polarity. A few of my findings have been used in the case histories chapter in this book.

Attempting to progress through a life that is defined only by the retrograde influence of the South Node is tantamount to a lifetime of severe discontent; being exposed to this lack of awareness places the soul in a no-win situation. I use the term "retrograde" loosely because the South Node signifies a lunar point of potentially spent energy, and yet its power and influence is immense. Furthermore, the South Node is a vital and influential facet in the natal chart because its purpose is one that is meant to kick-start the North Node into action, meaning its energy infuses and stimulates it.

Similar to planets in retrograde motion, the South Node represents a point of continued contemplation, pacification, and conciliation. However, it must be *stressed* that the South Node does *not* in any way signify the soul's innate calling. The South Node is a karmic echo reminding us of our previous experiences and achievements. It is a cosmic vessel accrued with an abundance of knowledge. The South Node has been cosmically designed for the purpose of *transference* and *integration*, wherein the release and transference of karmic energy from the South Node is then integrated and purified in the cosmic filtration system of the North Node for the purpose of enhanced future direction. According to Robert Jansky, "the prospect of illness and disease is *reinforced* when the North Node potential is not recognized."

So, for the soul to experience purification and purpose, we must transfer and integrate the knowledge and energy of the South Node into the empty unfamiliar recesses of the North Node. Once the knowledge is successfully stored, the calling of the North Node begins resonating at maximum volume and we begin to awaken to the now-familiar sounds of this transcendent lunar vibration, familiar as in "I remember this intimate calling." Only when this South Node transference-integration procedure is complete will the exploits associated with the multidimensional North Node become successful.

North Node pursuits, associated with early learning experiences or unconscious choices, will ultimately fail if the knowledge and experiences of the South Node have not yet been integrated insofar as they are *misrepresentative* of the divine plan. Contrary to the importance of the Nodes, the natal chart blueprint of planetary interplay, which includes the transits, *can* often pinpoint and determine when the transference-integration process is complete. Saturn and Pluto transits to the Nodes are especially relevant.

The natal chart configuration has been compiled by your soul to either facilitate or obfuscate the transference of Nodal energy depending on the level of karma that needs to be understood. Speaking also as a past-life therapist, I have ascertained that individuals who are born with either the Moon or Jupiter conjunct the Ascendant or Midheaven, for example, seem to become aware of the Nodal calling much sooner than those with Mercury or Mars. Mercury tends to get embroiled in a whirlwind of self-analysis, and Mars has a few personalized conflicts to overcome.

In addition, those individuals who have little or no planetary connection to the primary angles, including the North Node, will be more inclined to create disharmony within the soul as it synchronizes separately with the South Node associated safety net. Interestingly, this observation has frequently come to the forefront in astrological Node consultation. Also, all aspects to the Nodes need to be taken into consideration when observing the potential likelihood of Nodal transference.

Once the transference integration process is complete the Nodal polarity will effectively become transposed in energy coordination that acts similarly to the effects of planets in harmonic mutual reception. Likewise, once the Nodes have become an integrated polarity and their energies are utilized for the purpose of progression. Illness and disease may become redundant factors as the physical body is purged by the spiritual cleansing of the combined Nodal polarity.

DMP, Karma and South Node Transformation

Throughout this book you will read several references to DMP: *Deep Memory Process*. Hence, Deep Memory Process is a safe and effective form of healing that is used to explore our own past-life memories; it is also used to resolve emotional and psychological blockages that can profoundly affect out present-day *health* and happiness.[1] DMP works hand-in-hand with evolutionary and medical astrology, and is especially effective when we need to fully understand the evolutionary objective of the Moon's South Node.

Deep Memory Process is the ideal tool to use as an alternative measure to conventional regression therapy, especially when we choose to work with the cyclic energy field of the South Node. DMP methodology is essentially a natural form of healing that releases latent impasses that are more often than not subconsciously locked in that part of the soul that is symbolized by the South Node.

Hard aspects to the South Node, especially from those planets commonly referred to as the malefics, Mars and Saturn, or any of the outer planets; these indicate energy blockages caused by past life trauma within the psyche. Hard aspects can often determine soul fragmentation, especially when Neptune and Pluto (the cosmic brothers in arms so to speak) configure in the karmic equation.[2] The degrees of aspect orbs can often determine the severity of soul fragmentation; this is an area of astrological expertise that will be covered in greater detail in my forthcoming publication *Lunar Nodal Connections*.

Planets in dignity, hence *detriment* or *fall*, especially when aspected to the Nodes, denote a further imbalance of energy within these lunar points. Mercury in Pisces and Pluto in Libra when aspected to the Nodes for example would indicate a veil of naivety surrounding the soul that proved to be troublesome in a past life or lives. These awkward planetary configurations would denote detrimental service to others and the avoidance of positive opportunity; instead being drawn into toxic situations and scenarios, both of which are damaging to the soul, these are issues that need addressing in the here and now. Pluto and its polarity especially when aspected to the Nodes and Saturn can determine past life illness and disease.

If difficult aspects have been identified, the soul needs to be purged of these past-life dilemmas in order for the North Node to become a source of potent mastery. Left *untreated*, these energy blockages can, in some cases, result in mental and physical illness. This is why the South Node influence is one of the most difficult areas of our life to purge and get to grips with psychologically.

Despite popular consensus I believe that the South Node emphasizes a powerful *healing* point in the birth chart, especially when located at zero degrees or conjoining an angle such as the Ascendant or IC, or alternatively when occupying an angular house such as the first and fourth.

The Karmic Bundle

It has been pointed out, especially in Vedic astrology, that the South Node is an indication of the karmic weight the soul is carrying. Hypothetically, it would suggest that the soul is particularly burdened when the South Node works its influence from a *weighty*, dense-matter sign such as Taurus, Leo, or Sagittarius; after all, the Bull, Lion, and Centaur are considered heavyweights and are associated with survival tendencies. So we could surmise that the soul carries with it much baggage, depending in part upon aspects. However, this is not to say that the other signs indicate lighter karma. They don't. On the contrary, they are merely an extenuation of the karmic load.

The kind of baggage (whether it has been neatly and tightly bundled or remains loosely tied) is almost always determined by the heavier aspects to the South Node such as squares and sesquiquadrates, especially from the likes of Mars, Saturn, and Pluto. Also, if the South Node is located in Pisces or in a sign such as Libra or Cancer in hard aspect to the Ascendant or IC, escapist tendencies such as alcohol issues were prevalent in a past life or lives, whereby the Nodal placing would point to the continuation of ill health.

Multiple Dimensions of Consciousness

Try to imagine the South Node as a doorway or portal to a past life. If in the birth chart the South Node is heavily aspected, especially by conjunction, a past life interconnected echo or karmic familiarity needs addressing. As previously indicated, the purpose of DMP is to gently release latent transpersonal images from the soul that are channeled through the matrix of the South Node energy field for the sole purpose of healing, almost like an evolutionary journey through the photospheric archives of the soul.

According to Jungian writer Jolande Jacobi, "the soul has many masks." In my opinion this is a perfect description of the South Node cloak of multiple identities and dimensions. Good and bad, positive and negative, are all a part of the soul's karmic learning curvature of experience, and the key to unlocking the South Node requires a delicate balance of self-understanding, self-realization and self-acceptance.[3] When working with the South Node it is vitally important to factor in the karmic influence and potentiality of the evolutionary planet Pluto.

In many cases the South Node represents a menagerie of positive opportunities for evolutionary expansion, or opening up a single channel of observation within the soul's three-dimensional field of vision. In other words, the South Node can act like a karmic lens magnifying a stream of energy from past lives (the type of energy is dependant on the strength of aspects from other planets, especially Mars, Saturn, and Pluto). Moreover, the potential for soul expansion is particularly strong if the South Node is located in Pluto's polarity house, or alternatively if it is aspected to a planet that occupies Pluto's polarity point, such as Jupiter or Neptune via a conjunction, and particularly via a quintile aspect.

Quintiles and bi-quintiles are evolutionary aspects that invariably get little recognition. These aspects work well with the soul's energy when it needs to relinquish karmic baggage via the

South Node's energy exit point. Quintiles and bi-quintiles are also healing aspects, assisting the chakras in their healing process after the onset of illness and disease. These aspects can be likened to the natal chart's supply of medicine, especially when the South Node is positively aspected to the Sun, Moon, or Venus.

In addition, if the South Node is aspected to Pluto's polarity point by way of an evolutionary aspect the soul possesses enormous potential for spiritual progression. Working with a quintile aspect in this way provides an immense opportunity for the soul to conjoin with the futuristic energy point of the North Node. Interestingly, in numerology both the quintile and bi-quintile equate as the number nine, similar to the opposition (180 degrees), square and semi-square (90 and 45 degrees, respectively) and conjunction (360 degrees). A quintile is an aspect of 72 degrees orb (7+2 = 9). The bi-quintile is an aspect of 144 degrees orb (1+4+4 = 9). Numerology determines number nine as an evolutionary or spiritual number ruled by Pluto, thus expressing its spiritual principles and intentions through its actions. Nines have the potential for teaching, artistry and healing, which is the very essence of the quintile aspect.

Alternatively, if the South Node is aspected to Pluto's polarity by way of a square, the potential for evolutionary expansion paints a very different picture. (Squares and conjunctions to the Nodes and the polarity points are discussed further on.)

The South Node and the Bardo

According to ancient Tibetan Buddhism the bardo is a conscious state of awareness situated between the Earth-plane and the spiritual spheres; essentially these spheres act like spiritual stepping stones that lead us back to the universal divine or Godhead.[4] The soul's transition into the bardo is determined solely by the type of death that has been incurred; for example, whether death was peaceful or traumatic and whether it had been orchestrated by illness.

Meanwhile it is important to stipulate that the word *death* is nothing but a Westernized modern-day metaphor brought about through misunderstandings and fear-based doctrines. More precisely, we don't die; we are simple reborn into another dimension or state of consciousness. Even today a significant percentage of the populace, especially throughout Western culture, possess little or *no* faith. Greater still are those numbers of people who quite categorically *do not* believe in an afterlife state in any shape or form. This is one reason why illness is prevalent throughout western societies.

More important, when fear is carried into the bardo state it has often been caused by harrowing thoughts, distressing affirmations, and regret, which also occurs at the point of death, depending on the quality of the soul's departure from the physical plane. Therefore, to successfully heal in the bardo state, meaning to rid the soul of all Earth-plane vibrations and progress onward into the spiritual spheres, the soul must have successfully completed its evolutionary journey toward spiritual growth. Interestingly, and according to many past life therapists, illness and disease are the most common factors that draw the soul back into incarnation.

If a soul has died of a terminal illness it often decides that it must return to acquire some kind of realization to why it happened; so, in other words, it feels there is still unfinished business to take care of. In retrospect, the soul must return to a state of recognition of its spiritual potential, thus furthering the development of its higher beliefs or consciousness in order to attain absolution. Likewise, the soul must have developed a realization of the journey ahead to avoid these past life pitfalls—a journey that will encompass eventual and ultimate spiritual awareness.

More important, during its lengthy intermittent transition upon the physical plane the soul must have successfully attained peace, tranquillity, and harmony by relinquishing the discord that is associated with illness and disease. In addition, the soul must have developed an everlasting faith, coupled with an acceptance to the purpose of the divine will. These attributes can only be attained when the North Node potential has been fully realized and its energy fully enveloped by the soul. Equally these attributes can be attained, in part, when Chiron and its multifaceted influence has been worked on and thus fully realized.

The soul must have finalized at least ninety percent of its karma, making certain that no additional karma has been created throughout the current incarnation. Illness and disease are contributing factors in the build up of karma.

Once the soul transcends the energy field of the Earth plane and successfully makes it into the spiritual spheres it will be gradually purified of the reverberations that mark the soul's evolutionary tally of illnesses and diseases. Only then will the "heaviness" that it has carried around for millennia and throughout its myriad of incarnations will be lifted as it gradually begins to move closer towards the unconditional love that gracefully emanates from the divine, which forever encompasses the soul's eternal light of bliss.

A Profound State of Unconsciousness

It is my belief, and the belief of other like-minded souls, that the reason for the endless spiral of global degradation and apathy, not to mention the proliferating levels of illness, that are evident on the planet today is caused primarily by a cataclysm that occurred millions of years ago. It is the last in a line of cataclysms, and if humanity doesn't start altering its perception of life then it will happen again within three Pluto generations (about seventy-five years). Unfortunately, the side effects from the last cataclysm have left us with a sense of disconnection (another cause of illness). This disconnection factor has essentially placed us on different levels of progression. This is one reason why there is so much hate, prejudice, fear, apathy and solace in the world currently.

The Moon's South Node

The diversifying levels of consciousness that are forever manifesting on Earth are similar to the opposite ends of a magnet that can be likened to the North and South Node polarity fields or divides. Despite popular opinion we are not meant to be on different levels of progression, realistically speaking; we are all meant to be at the same evolutionary juncture.[5]

The Wider Influence of the South Node

This profound state of unconsciousness began millennia ago when we left the Godhead. This was essentially the beginning of this current disillusioned wave of incoherency that *has* and *continues* to blight the very fabric of humankind. As we are all one big collective consisting of many Pluto soul groups within that collective, we are meant to be operating on the same soul frequency. This glitch in the cosmic timeline has occurred, in part, by the soul as it *drags* itself back into incarnation because of those dying thoughts or affirmations that we have spoken about. Alternatively, it is because of an obsession such as fixing something—Pluto's unfinished business factor.

Obsessions come in many guises. Today some of the most prevalent obsessions are physical glamor and greed, and this is partly because we live in the age of the celebrity. An amazing number of people believe they can take their wealth with them once their time on the Earth plane draws to its natural conclusion. Unresolved sexuality, gender issues, and gluttony are other classic symptoms of obsession, all of which lead to ill health, and so invariably the soul will come back for another stab at what it believes it has missed. Therefore, every time obsessions and karmic-based thoughts take hold in the bardo, they prevent the soul from raising its evolutionary vibration and progressing.

In effect, the South Node represents unfinished business in the realm of physical incarnation as well as in the bardo state. In some cases the soul doesn't actually realize that it has passed over. And so here lies the ultimate paradox of karmic stagnation, which in turn orchestrates the classic unconscious state of perpetual unawareness—superior issues in the bardo; in effect this can be likened to a kind of spiritual illness.

As well as the obvious factors, the South Node is also a reflection of the soul's take on the bardo state of consciousness. If the native has subconsciously *refused* to take that leap of faith into the North Node potential and instead becomes complacently trapped in the South Node safety net, the chances are the soul won't make it past the bardo state upon death, which is, in my opinion, another form of illness. It is the recognition of the North Node and the faith that needs to be developed as a result of this lunar point that allows the soul to cross into the spiritual spheres.

The South Node not only symbolizes physical incarnation on the Earth plane but also the varying diverse states of consciousness that have effectively played out in the bardo state. So if we don't finalize the effects of the South Node upon the physical plane, its influence remains strong, manifesting as unfinished business. As a result the soul drags itself back into incarnation and the repetitious cycle of karma begins once more.

Ascertaining the Soul's Vibration

Aspects, especially conjunctions, to the Nodes and their rulers, will ultimately determine the soul's journey, whether it is one that is blighted by ill health and repetition or one that has the potential for harmony and realization (a planet or planets that conjoin the North Node will naturally oppose the South Node).

Here the conjunction is the superior force giving more nuance and bravado to the soul's proposed plan making it far easier to realise the potential of the North Node energy. The opposition to the South Node will act as a release once the past-life knowledge has been successfully extracted; hence a preverbal handshake is then needed in order for the onset of healing to begin. Unfortunately, what makes the South Node vibrate as unfinished business is when this scenario is reversed and the North Node is the one that is released long before its potential has been realized. This often occurs because of conjunctions to the South Node and/or its ruler.

A planet or planets in square formation will of course be in simultaneous aspect to both of the Nodes, creating the Nodal t-square or Nodal Grand Cross configuration. In the case of the t-square the polarity of the apex planet becomes the focal point for manifestation. These configurations create impasses and will render the individual with the difficult task of not knowing which direction to take—North or South.

Quintiles and bi-quintiles to the Nodes and their rulers can be extremely favorable, as mentioned earlier, providing their gentle vibrations are contemplated in the correct manner. This evolutionary aspect can successfully point the soul in the right direction and inone that necessitates futuristic growth. All aspects are potentially *positive*; it all depends on our perception and determination to act in accordance with our individual karma.

Endnotes

[1]DMP (Deep Memory Process) was founded by *Roger Woolger*, the late Jungian analyst and author of the seminal book *Other Lives, Other Selves*. Practised by some evolutionary astrologers including Patricia L.Walsh, DMP is an extremely effective form of self-healing.

[2]Ancient mythology determines that Neptune and Pluto were bothers. They are in fact both water planets. The astrologer Betty Gosling refers to them as the "terrible twins."

[3]According to Carl Jung "we do not become enlightened by imagining beings of light, but by making the darkness conscious."

[4]In order to attain more information on the spiritual spheres I

recommend reading *The Joseph Communications: Your Life after Death* by Michael G. Reccia, published by Band of Light Media. Interestingly there are twelve spheres, as there are houses in the birth chart. Can this be significant in some way? The twelfth sphere is the entrance point to the divine.

[5] A notion that is further verified in the *Tibetan Book of the Dead*.

CHAPTER 6

The Moon's North Node: Illumination

"In Evolutionary Astrology it is said that to evolve from any natal planetary position to its polarity point is to move from Karma to Dharma, which is, at its apex, personal will aligned with divine will."—Patricia L. Walsh

THE NORTH/SOUTH NODE POLARITY DESCRIBES the *prima materia*—the essential building blocks that construct, support and fabricate the essential journey of life. However, to fully understand the evolutionary dynamics of the birth chart we must first understand the position, purpose and potential of the Moon's Nodes, paying particular attention to the North Node, the soul's navigational compass.

The North Node: the Distant Calling

The North Node is in *exaltation* in Gemini and in its *fall* in Sagittarius, which is the reverse polarity of the South Node.

Before we begin it is important to stipulate that the planets are interconnected with the Nodes, and in particular to the North Node, even in the absence of aspects. Therefore, it is important to remember that every planet in the natal chart represents an *association* or *affinity* with the North Node in some obligatory way; but mainly the planets are connected to the Nodes for the purpose of potential, realization, and aspiration. However, viewing it from another perspective we could imply that the North Node represents the head of the planetary/karmic board of hierarchies. So how important is this North Node influence and what does it represent?

Similar to its lunar polarity, the South Node the North Node is not a planet; it is a point in the heavens. The North Node augments our cosmic blueprint for the evolutionary transition of the soul (hence our individualized divine plan) that predetermines the purpose, the potentialality, and the evolutionary calling of reincarnation, and its significance for the underlying influence of progression.

Metaphorically, the North Node is the underlining yet powerful vibration that reverberates ten-fold through the intricate chasms of the soul. But our recognition and awareness of this divine form of guidance is invariably blotted out or hidden from view. Moreover, the North Node is the temporal seed that is slowly and subtly germinated through the Earth-plane influence of linearity, which comes under the rulership of Saturn—karma and physical incarnation. Unaware of the divine plan that is a representation of the multidimensional facet of the North Node, a large percentage of the world's population is *still* influenced by the familiarity of their South Node safety net as discussed in Chapter 5. As a result many human beings are missing the opportunity to hear the distant but direct calling of their soul. Principally, the calling and the ideology of the North Node signifies an area of life we are meant to explore.[1]

If every human being upon this planet observed the innate calling of his or her soul illness, disease would be stamped out in a very short time.

Achieving Evolutionary Balance via the North Node

Evolutionary balance signifies a karmic impulse to purge events and search for situations that will ultimately bring life back into perspective, and into the familiar domain of self-awareness. Alternatively, when we experience a complete imbalance within the psyche it confirms wholeheartedly that we are indeed out of control. When human beings express themselves both *objectively* and *inclasticly* from the South Node safety net an imbalance will occur within the psyche, thus indicating the lack of cohesion within the Nodal polarity. This is known affectionately as the swing of the South Node pendulum.

In our personal lives we continually work toward finding a physical, psychological, and spiritual balance (balance will only occur when the energy of the North and South Node becomes integrated and operates as a single and enhanced form of consciousness). As a whole, the North Node helps us to balance our personal desires, needs, and ambitions in order to feel a sense of satisfaction. The North Node helps us to determine what we truly *need* to enhance our lives as opposed to what we *want*, which invariably becomes a source of hindrance.

Drawing upon the influence of the Nodes and their aspects may determine a past life where individuals gave too much of themselves, meaning they gave too much energy and to their own detriment. Pluto's sign, position, and aspects would more often than not point to this dispositional imbalance. This being the case, the North Node would no doubt be in a position in the natal chart that would indicate the need to accommodate other people's energies in order to achieve a physical, psychological, and spiritual balance (such as the first house).

However, from its seventh house position (opposing the first) the South Node would highlight a wealth of shared recourses, knowledge, and values that the soul acquired in past lives, so in effect this should ideally help the individual to build up and strengthen his or her own sense of personal worth (first house) in order to achieve the evolutionary polarity balance of the Nodes.

Therefore, in retrospect, this evolutionary balance centers heavily on the North Node axis point of the birth chart with the inclusion of Pluto, especially when Pluto is in aspect to the

Nodes. Once a balance has been *achieved* the karma or knowledge that is locked within the South Node is finally *released* and *integrated* into the North Node.

The Polarity of the Soul

According to Heraclitus "the opposite is good for you."

Just as this repetitive and often mundane cycle of incarnation symbolizes unfinished business, the Moon's North Node is in effect the absolution factor that can help us to break the cycle of incarnation, and this is why the South Node polarity point is so important.

As indicated earlier, the North Node can assist with the transition into the spiritual spheres once physical incarnation has concluded. But in order for this transition to be successful the soul must have relinquished every bit of karma that is suppressed within the psyche and the individual must have taken advantage of every opportunity that was available via the North Node energy field.

The transition from the physical plane to the astral (spiritual) plane doesn't have to be distressing. It is only distressing when the cycle of opportunity has been forfeited. If the potential of the North Node has been realized and taken advantage of, then its positive effects will remain with the soul long after the physical termination from the Earth plane. The soul will be then become evenly balanced and *free* from illness and disease.

The Transiting Lunar Nodes

Nodal returns occur every eighteen years.

North Node Transit Conjunctions

Sun: Generally speaking, this transit denotes a time of increased success and enlightenment based on the house the Sun occupies in the individual's chart. It also represents an awakening of the ego.

Moon: Here the emotions become the focus of awareness. The feminine side of the psyche needs to be expressed more, and even women can operate to a greater degree from the masculine side. Check the house placement of the Moon for the area that the attention will be most likely noticed.

Mercury: Sudden and unexpected changes are likely to occur. There may also be more nervous energy than normal. Consequently you may not feel like talking too much mainly because your brain is working in overdrive mode.

Venus: During this time romantic and financial situations may be sent into a cooling off period for the purpose of contemplation. Contemplation is not a negative issue; it implies that a reassessment of any situation is necessary.

Mars: Physical activities are inclined to expand under this transit. Talking on too many chores and pushing too hard is also a likely possibility. Self-centeredness is also something that needs to be kept in check.

Jupiter: Musings of a philosophical or religious nature could be activated at this time. Money matters need to be kept in check, especially where overindulgence is concerned. It is also a time to break free of conventional habits and disciplines.

Saturn: During this transit there will be an opportunity to learn more about the changes in the rules that may have been *overlooked* in the past. Look to older and wiser individuals for insight, advice and guidance.

Chiron: Building a bridge between the objective mind and the subconscious mind for the purpose of understanding the fundamental plan of the North Node. The purpose is to gain valuable insight into the soul's wound and to project the wound *outwardly* for the purpose of self-attainment and realisation.[2]

Uranus: The ego will be divided through this transit. Ego works best when it has been *purged* of self-righteous beliefs. This is also an opportunity to scrutinize the potential of the higher mind because spiritual endeavours will present themselves. This is a time to release blocked energy from within the psyche for the purpose of self-canalization.

Neptune: The represents the dissolving of the ego and transcendence onto the plane of spiritual enlightenment. There will be an opportunity now to balance the dark recesses of the mind with the eternal light of the soul for the purpose of healing.

Pluto: Transformation is likely on the evolutionary journey toward soul ascension. This transit denotes the destroying of old habits and life patterns. Changes are likely in long-term financial affairs such as mortgages and pensions.

North Node: This signifies a karmic transition period. Eighteen years, growth through past lessons learned; thirty-six years, comprehension of balance between self-ego and relationships; fifty-four years, new period of identity growth with increased grounding and wisdom; seventy-two years, compulsion to impart wisdom to others; and ninety years, coming to terms with the life cycle which is based on self-earned wisdom. Remember also that the transiting South Node is conjunct the natal South Node and can *draw* the energy away from growth if the individual chooses to go in the South node direction.

South Node: This signifies a development period. Nine years, the beginning of emotional growth as an independent being; twenty-seven years, awareness involving the significance of relationships; forty-five years, reformation of self through others; and sixty-three years, redefining personal priorities.

South Node Transit Conjunctions

Sun: Denotes a feeling of despair or soul fragmentation. Marks an inability to grasp current events and circumstances, particularly in areas related to the house that the Sun occupies.

Moon: There is a likelihood of depression or feelings of isolation can emerge during this transit. Such things as blocked emotions remain *unclear*. There may also be problems in the area of fertility, whether physical, imaginative, or creative. Health issues should also be addressed.

Mercury: Denotes feelings of ineffective communication or possibly unfocused thinking patterns. There is an inability to cope with sudden changes and environmental issues. This can be a difficult transit.

Venus: Karmic based relationships could develop *suddenly* during this transit. This can be a time of sudden financial loss. Misguided energies concerning finances or one-to-one relationships may alter the soul's journey.

Mars: During this transit health issues are prevalent. Physical blockages will tend to increase, causing weakness and listlessness in the psyche. Be aware of accidents and be willing to adopt more caution.

Jupiter: Belief systems are likely to come under scrutiny during this time. Financial gains could be relevant, but take care not to walk over others in the pursuit of financial reward.

Saturn: Significant environmental changes and shifting circumstances are likely to occur in the event of a death. However, death is not necessarily physical; it can be an emotional or psychological transition. The emotional upheaval of leaving something behind that is considered to be important is similar to the transition of death.

Chiron: Unclear thinking and the need to relate to past hurts become evident when the South Node transits Chiron. Karmic-related illness can also be a problem, especially where the digestion is concerned. Contemplation and clarity are needed here.

Uranus: Sudden shifts in consciousness are likely to occur under this transit of the South Node. A feeling of isolation is also likely as the ego divides and fragments, caused primarily by the presence of past life energies. Accidents can also be an issue.

Neptune: Memories and images of past life scenarios will surface under this transit. Pay particular attention to dreams. Unfocused thoughts and actions are likely to be a cause for concern. Deceit and deception can also rear up and take charge.

Pluto: A fear of change is instilled in the psyche and when change occurs it invariably comes at a price. This is a karmic issue and the South Node is indicating that change was most likely resisted in a past life. During this transit Pluto is attempting to remove the shackles of fear from the soul.

Conclusion

Solely dependent on the level of conscious awareness attained in the current incarnation, the North Node often remains an *uncertain configuration* to the soul. However, failure to recognize and understand the purpose of the divine plan (which is representative of the North Node) is often the result of past life familiarities and teachings, and is emphasized by powerful aspects to the South Node.

Therefore, spiritual pursuits and studying such intricacies as *human design* can help to unlock the cosmic mysteries of the lunar North Node axis.[3] Throughout my studies of Nodal influences upon the psyche I have discovered that during Nodal returns the body seems to become susceptible to illness and disease. During Nodal returns it's almost as if a psychic déjà vu element is present bringing forth past life issues that are not finalised, emphasising the illness factor.

Endnotes

[1]Reference to the astrologer Laurence Hillman.

[2]The term "soul's wound" is implied as merely a metaphor. It is our distance from being *soulful* that makes us feel the soul needs healing. Indeed, the soul is *perfect*.

[3]For more information concerning the human energy field I recommend visiting www.humandesignforusall.com

CHAPTER 7

Nodal Chart Interpretation

"The Nodal energy animates a chart and describes a course of purposeful action that gives life meaning."—
Kathy Allan

IN ORDER TO FULLY COMPREHEND the dynamics of the natal chart we must first understand the position and purpose of the Moon's Nodes and their ruling planets. Many astrologers, including myself, believe that the Nodes have great importance in the chart, and that a qualified expert is able to understand a person's health and general well-being simply by analyzing the Sun, Moon, and the position of the Nodes.

Try to imagine the South Node as the catalyst for the *trauma* of unfinished or unresolved business. Then try to imagine the North Node as the catalyst for *tragedy* associated with a fear of the unknown. Stepping through that cosmic doorway into an unfamiliar domain can bring tragedy, especially if there are still unresolved issues to resolve. Because unfinished business is associated with Pluto, tragedy can be about loss, endings, and even manifest as illness and disease, which will necessitate the prospect of further trauma. Working to consciously integrate the Nodes into its fully functional polarity will inspire new direction and spiritual realisation.

Someone once described my birth chart as being like a cosmic spider's web: intricate, precise, and with so many planetary exactitudes and with no escape through orbs. An accurate analysis! But consider if you will the potential and possibilities of a chart using the premise of *Lunar Nodal Connections*.

If we begin with the rulers of the Nodes as the starting points for chart interpretation and determine their influence on the rest of the chart, we can get a good foothold into ascertaining the evolutionary purpose and health of the individual. I have therefore used myself as the following case example for Nodal chart interpretation.

Evolutionary Purpose

The rulers of the Nodes hold the key to the purpose of the entire chart, and in my chart the rulers are Pluto and Venus. The North Node in Scorpio (Pluto) is posited between the Sun and Mercury in the tenth house of status, ambition, and career (the tenth house being ruled traditionally by Capricorn and Saturn). The Sun and Mercury oppose the South Node in Taurus in the fourth house, Taurus is ruled by Venus, and the fourth house is traditionally ruled by Cancer and the Moon. This planetary Nodal configuration is square the Vertex (the angle of destiny) conjunct Uranus in Leo (detrimental) from the eighth house cusp ruled by Black Moon Lilith and Pluto.[1] Uranus is also the ruler of astrology. Venus, the ruler of the South Node, rises via a tight conjunction from the Ascendant and is the accidental ruler of the third, fourth, and fifth houses, which are traditionally ruled by Mercury, Moon, and Sun. Venus also rules the IC.

Pluto in Virgo (detrimental) occupies the eighth house (its traditional home), which is ruled accidentally by the Sun and the modern ruler of Virgo, Chiron. Furthermore, Pluto opposes the Moon in the second house in Pisces within a one-degree orb in an applied aspect (the second house is ruled traditionally by Venus). The Moon's sign of Cancer rules the seventh house, which is potentially ruled by Black Moon Lilith as opposed to the traditionally held view of Venus. Venus also makes a tight

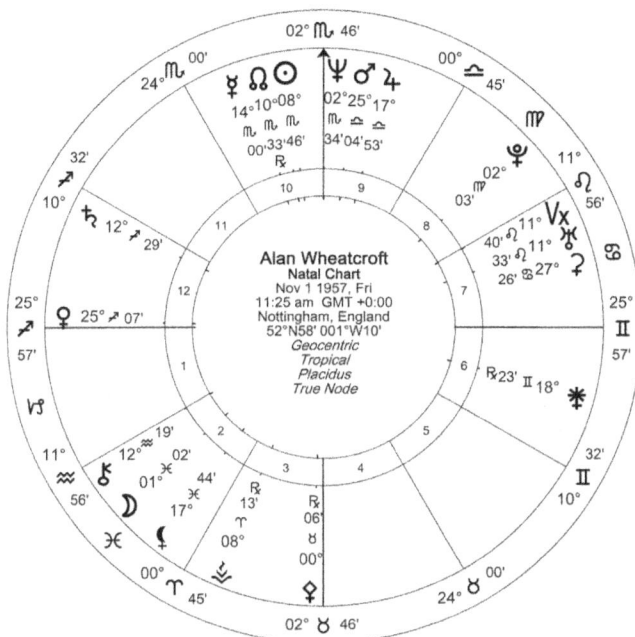

Alan Wheatcroft
Natal Chart
Nov 1 1957, Fri
11:25 am GMT +0:00
Nottingham, England
52°N58' 001°W10'
Geocentric
Tropical
Placidus
True Node

sextile to Mars in Libra conjunct Jupiter, also in Libra (seventh house). Chiron occupies Aquarius (ruled by Uranus) and opposes Uranus from the second to the seventh house polarity; once again the influence of Venus and Black Moon Lilith is evident, and the Sun rules Uranus's sign of Leo (detrimental). Saturn occupies Jupiter's sign of Sagittarius and Jupiter occupies its rulership house (the ninth). The Nodes also link into a Grand Cross configuration with Chiron and Uranus. As you can see the rulers of the Nodes are very prominent.

Next we'll consider Neptune's influence in the chart. Some esoteric astrologers believe Neptune to be the higher octave vibration of Venus. In my chart, Neptune is sextile Pluto and trine the Moon in Neptune's own sign of Pisces from the Venus-ruled second house. Neptune shrouds the Midheaven in Scorpio (Pluto) and is in wide conjunction to the Sun. Venus occupies Neptune's traditional domain (the twelfth house) along with Saturn, and Saturn nudges Uranus in a separating trine. Black Moon Lilith is also in the second house in Pisces (traditionally ruled by Venus).

General Summary

Venus and Pluto are the focal points for the entire chart. What this means is that I have had to break free from outdated family traditions, family values, and surroundings that have caused an element of *trauma*, especially in early life (the South Node from the fourth and the Moon's opposition to Pluto), and find my place in the world for the purpose of evolutionary transformation (Pluto and the tenth house stellium), which has orchestrated a wealth of personal *tragedy*.[2]

The life path indicates a career in writing, especially astrology (the tenth house stellium and Mercury, which rules the Descendant square Uranus and the Vertex). It also means that by using my Neptunian lofty idealism I am able to write fantasy stories coupled with an astrological theme. Also, following a lifetime of challenges and merely surviving (Taurus South Node), I must make myself financially viable, which is the ultimate life challenge (Venus, money, and Pluto, mega money). Astrology will open up other opportunities for personal and spiritual advancement, which in turn will allow me to discover who I am and my heavenly purpose within the divinely oriented universe; hence, the powerful Neptune chart connection.

The rulers of the Nodes (Pluto and Venus) also influence my personal numerology numbers, which are as follows:

- The life path number is 7, ruled by Neptune; and Neptune's sign is Scorpio (Pluto).

- The soul expression number is 3, ruled by Jupiter; and Jupiter's sign is Libra (Venus or Black Moon Lilith).

- The soul urge number is 5, ruled by Mercury; and Mercury's sign is Scorpio (Pluto).

- The destiny number is 7, ruled by Neptune; and Neptune's sign is Scorpio (Pluto).

- The karmic number is 0, ruled by the Sun; and the Sun's sign is Scorpio (Pluto).

Health Summary

The rulers of the Nodes (Venus and Pluto) can also have a profound affect in medical astrology, as my personal example demonstrates.

With the tremendous quadrature of planets in water signs—the Sun in Scorpio, Moon in Pisces, Mercury in Scorpio, Neptune in Scorpio conjunct the Scorpio Midheaven and its sextile to Pluto (another water planet), and Pluto's opposition to the Moon—my internal system is heavily "water-logged." This configuration is related to severe congestion in my sinus cavities and abdominal stress in the bowel region, causing IBS (Irritable Bowel Syndrome), especially during those periods when there are transiting triggers. Literally, all this fluid must come out somewhere.

The Sun's square to Uranus has caused a lifetime of sudden bowel spasms, with Scorpio ruling the bowels. The Sun also receives aspects from the Moon, Mercury, and Venus, and Uranus receives applied sesquiquadrates from the Ascendant and Venus. The Moon's opposition to Pluto has been responsible for a multitude of nasal conditions such as frequent infections in the mucus membranes (Moon), rhinitis, and catarrh. The Moon also receives an applied sesquiquadrate from Jupiter and a trine from Mars and Neptune. Pluto receives a semi-square from Jupiter and an applied quintile from Mercury and a trine from Venus, which have enhanced these distressed conditions.

Then, in 2009, I became seriously ill with pancreatitis (Pluto ruling the pancreas and Virgo ruling the gallbladder). At the time of diagnosis and putting aside the minor aspect triggers, particularly inconjunctions and sesquiquadrates, Pluto, Mars, and Saturn were exactly conjunct Pluto, and Neptune was conjunct the Moon within a four-degree applied orbital radius. After making a brief recovery, in 2011, pancreatitis struck again, and aside from other significators the main culprit was Neptune conjunct the Moon and opposition Pluto, along with the untimely inclusion of Mars and Jupiter (liver).

Neptune rules hospitals and that is where I found myself again after being admitted on the seventh day of the fourth month—seven being ruled by Neptune and four ruled by Saturn—and I do have Saturn in Neptune's twelfth house of incarceration. In addition, and on that fateful day, I experienced a severe gallbladder attack and died for seven minutes (Neptune again), and the time of death was nine o'clock—death and nine being ruled by Pluto. However, in that seven minutes I had the most profound, beautiful and heart-moving near death experience that is hard to describe. I cannot recount the love and the sense of awe and euphoria I felt during those seven minutes, with euphoria being Neptune. It was something I needed to have because the experience changed me forever.

The following day I undertook a lengthy operation to remove an obstruction from my abdomen and widen the bile ducts—operations falling under the rulership of Mars. Since then and after making a few life changes, I have made a full recovery. As I write this I am still under that Neptune transit to the Moon and Pluto, and I can only express my thanks that I my eyes have been opened, giving me renewed vision. As for my waterlogged system, I now live near the sea and breathing in salty air has helped to neutralize this condition.

Endnotes

[1]Betty Gosling, an astrologer and dear friend, ascertains that Black Moon Lilith is the true ruler of Libra. This hypothesis could be correct as Libra is the *oddity* of the zodiac; and when I say oddity I mean that the sign is 'mechanical' as opposed to the mythical symbolisations of both the human and animal king-

dom. Also, Venus is more connected to financial matters, especially as its polarity is Pluto, and nature, than that of personal, social and corporate interaction.

[2]Astrologers Ivy Goldstein-Jacobson and Komilla Sutton believe that the Nodes of the Moon bring *Trauma* and *Tragedy*.

Nodal Chart Interpretation

Part 3

Case Studies

CHAPTER 8

Bursitis

*"In that book which is my memory, on the first page is
the chapter marking the day which I met you appears the
words here begins a new life."*—Dante

ONCE AN ILLNESS OR DISEASE culminates, or reaches its peak, it
invariably begins to wane or subside. Essentially this waning effect marks a point of *realization*, and out of that realization comes
a new beginning. This new beginning accentuates the Plutonian
fable of the Phoenix rising out of the ashes of its earlier life.

This first of the case studies examines a typical breakdown
within the body's immune system, which has been caused by a
disruption to the flow of information (chakral energy) around
the body, both physical and mental. Subsequently we will see
this all-too-familiar commonality occurring throughout all of
the case study chapters and throughout every kind of illness and
disease especially throughout western civilization.

In the first case study the blockage in question was indicated
by a series of inherent oppositions, that as a result caused the
onset and development of greater trochanteric pain syndrome
(bursitis), and thus inflammation of the bursa.

Greater trochanteric pain syndrome (GTPS), also known as
trochanteric bursitis, is inflammation of the trochanteric bursa,
a part of the hip. The bursa is situated adjacent to the femur, between the insertion of the gluteus medius and gluteus minimus

muscles and into the greater trochanter of the femur and the femoral shaft. Its functions as a shock absorber and lubricant for the movement of the muscles adjacent to it.

Occasionally the bursa can become inflamed, which causes it to become clinically *painful* and *tender*. This condition can also be a manifestation of rheumatoid arthritis or of an injury (often resulting from a twisting motion or from overuse), but sometimes arises for no obviously definable cause. The symptoms are pain in the hip region and tenderness over the upper part of the femur, which may result in the inability to walk correctly and lie in comfort on the affected side.[1]

Astrological Diagnosis

The rulers of the Nodes are opposing other significant planets. Mercury (ruler of the North Node) is opposing Pluto, and Jupiter (ruler of the South Node) is opposing the Moon, which is dogged by the fixed star Algol. The Nodes ruling the sixth and twelfth house polarity seem to suggest that the bursitis is an *overlapping* condition carried over from a past life.

The chart draws attention to many underlying factors (potential symptoms) that are essentially linked to this painful and unyielding illness. According to author Louise Hay, "bursitis is caused by repressed anger" and as a consequence life often loses its *sweetness* and piquancy. The fifth house is in my opinion the domain where the sweetness for life is expressed. Sweetness is a term that best describes a healthy, happy, and virulent heart, attributing to both the physical and spiritual heart; and the fifth house represents the heart. The chart shows the Moon and Jupiter intercepted from the fifth-eleventh house polarity in the fixed signs of Taurus and Scorpio, and the Moon is also conjunct the fixed star *Algol*—"the dark greater one." [2] The North Node (subsequent direction in life) is in the fifth house, which highlights the necessity to instill wholly new mental pathways in the crown chakral region and psychological well-being in the heart centre.

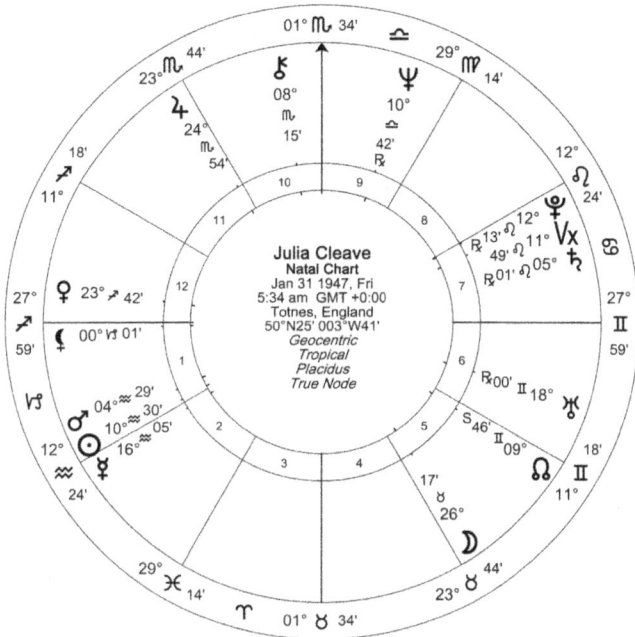

Julia Cleave
Natal Chart
Jan 31 1947, Fri
5:34 am GMT +0:00
Totnes, England
50°N25' 003°W41'
Geocentric
Tropical
Placidus
True Node

The Sun (ruler of the fifth) is the accidental ruler of the seventh and eighth house of interaction, transformation, and rebirth, and Pluto (the ruler of the eighth) is on the eighth house cusp. Interestingly, planets in this position are additionally significant to the rest of the chart, and it's almost as if planets located on cuspal points are taking a peak into an unknown realm. Pluto is also influenced by a sesquiquadrate from the Ascendant. Sagittarius rules the Ascendant and is the sign traditionally associated with the hips and thighs.

More significantly, the chart is intercepted by a series of oppositions that affect the first, seventh, second, and eighth house polarities. In effect, these opposition pointers are quite likely to be the main significators for bursitis, as well as other potential afflictions, including muscle deterioration. Several years previously the individual incurred a serious muscle tear, and also suffers from fibromyalgia (chronic fatigue syndrome). Technically, the bursa is a moving part, so its function is to act as a kind of muscle messenger, relaying information and energy to the muscles via the nervous system; therefore, the bursa must be categorized under the rulership of Mercury, which rules the fifth and sixth houses of vitality and health. Furthermore, Mercury is opposing Pluto the planet of genetic change and mutation.

Under the effects of this opposition the bursa can become indignant and *irritated* and therefore incredibly painful during times of significant cosmic transition. Thus, the transits activate Mercury's inability to understand Pluto's powerful message; after all, Mercury is merely the messenger of the cosmos and is unaware of the content of each message being delivered. In addition, Mercury's *stress factor* is heightened by the Sun's semisquare to Venus in Sagittarius; this configuration, along with the Sun-Mercury conjunction, places immense pressure on the bursa and the adjacent muscles.

Mercury and Uranus in mutual reception personify their effects and are joined by a trine and in mutual reception in a Grand Trine involving the Sun and Neptune. The supple and gentle effect of the Grand Trine would render the individual with an ability to heal, learn, and *aspire* toward greater mental aspirations and higher purpose, all for the greater good of humanity.

Mars's tight opposition to Saturn is likely to be the catalyst for painful bone and joint disorders, although it is never a good idea to determine individual significators as root causes. Nevertheless, the individual does suffer from overall joint pain and is also in the early stages of osteoporosis. As we determined earlier, the individual is continually afflicted by low levels of energy (fibromyalgia), which can be attributed to Saturn's crystallization effect decelerating Mars's energy flow restricting the energy that is being absorbed into the hips. As Mars frequents the first house, its rulership zone, energy is an integral and necessary part of the body's survival and natural healing process. Added to this is the Sun's opposition to Pluto, also from the first house, which indicates a low and degenerate metabolism.

The Aquarius stellium is interconnected by an orb of six degrees and according to author *Olivia Barclay*, six degrees interpreted in this way can symbolize *blockages*.[3] Traditionally speaking, Aquarius is said to represent the flow of the life force energy, and with the Sun in detriment at the heart of the stellium a blockage in the life force has become an overwhelming factor. Neptune's position from the ninth house with its sesquiquadrate to the Moon and semi-square to Jupiter also exemplifies the low energy situation.

Because of its ninth house position and connection to Sagittarius and Jupiter we can hypothesize that Neptune indicates a wasting disease that affects the hips or thighs. The individual also has a cystic liver, which is likely related to Jupiter's afflictions to Neptune and the Moon, and Jupiter is the chart ruler.

Prognosis

Although the individual has suffered from bursitis most of her life, similar to all life-debilitating ailments, there have been peaks and troughs throughout this condition. The most recent and possibly most lengthy flare-up occurred initially during the breakdown of her marriage. The culprits were most likely transiting Uranus in Pisces and Neptune in Aquarius in mutual reception. Neptune conjoined the chart's stellium of Aquarius planets from the first house and opposed Saturn and Pluto in the seventh, which I suspect indicated the inflammation to the bursa (Mars ruling inflammation). The bursa would have already been *weakened* prior to this by Neptune's transit of Capricorn, which would have *leaked* energy from this particular bodily area.

To cap it off, the heart center would have been suppressed further as Neptune formed a t-square to the Moon-Jupiter opposition, and this would most likely have been the catalyst for additional repressed anger. Uranus from its Pisces station was square natal Venus and the Ascendant, which in turn brought about a sudden, painful, and messy divorce that had long-term consequences on the individual's state of mind and is an issue that is still clearly evident today. In my opinion repressed anger is the main culprit that has unequivocally prevented the bursitis from healing.

The healing process would nonetheless be given a much-needed boost by Saturn's intermittent trine to Neptune.

The quadrature of planets in *fixed* signs clearly doesn't help the healing process—a fact that is also demonstrated by the individual's inability to let go and thus relinquish issues of an emotional and cerebral nature. Unless the repressed anger is purged, the chart clearly states that bursitis could very well be an ongoing issue that would affect the rest of this individual's life.

With the Moon conjoining Algol it will be a difficult task for this individual to *embrace* life's eternal sweetness. According to author *Reinhold Ebertin*, "it is very difficult to avoid accidents, severe injury, or debilitating illness if Algol is conjunct the Sun, Moon, or the Malefics." A damming prospect perhaps or a hidden opportunity maybe for spiritual growth. Either way, because of the fifth house interception, the abuse of power in past lives seems a relevant and circumspect hypothesis.

In order to determine the hidden meaning of illness we could assume that the bursitis could simply be acting as a grounding mechanism that would place the individual in a state of contemplation (Pluto). Subsequently this would allow the individual to *take stock* of her life circumstances and more importantly to listen to her heart's calling, which is a necessary cure for all types of illness.

Finally, the rulers of the Nodes (Mercury and Jupiter) determine that the poor quality of health has been carried over from past lives, as noted from the position of these planets in the chart, being disposed by Pluto and the Moon with Saturn ruling the first house. Hence, both the bursitis and fibromyalgia are merely conditions resulting from unfinished business in a mental health capacity, as Gemini and Sagittarius represent the polarity of mental cognation.

Finally, the reader will also observe from the chart that Gemini and Sagittarius are positioned on the sixth-twelfth house polarity, which is the polarity of health and karma.

Conclusion

After many consultations and regression therapy, Julia is now undergoing vibrational healing and sound wave therapy in Switzerland in order to treat the bursitis and the fibromyalgia. She is gradually getting her life back, and there has been a marked improvement in her health as well as her overall outlook.

Biorhythms

An important point to remember in is that illness and disease can still occur even though there are no evident transiting triggers. More often than not, illness and disease are the result of culminating or separating transits. However, if there are no triggers evident I would suggest checking the status of the lunar biorhythms. Biorhythm depletion is often the result of physical, mental, and spiritual degradation. Alternatively, it can be the catalyst for illness even in the absence of planetary triggers. It is a fact that the planets and the biorhythms *will* create a confluence of simultaneous energy that works together in complete synergy.

Endnotes

[1]Information courtesy of the *Medical Journal of Health and Well Being* published by Collins.
[2]Reinhold Ebertin named *Algol* "the dark greater one." Some believe Algol is the most evil star in the universe. Ebertin hypothesises that Algol is one of many dark stars that occupy the Algol system.
[3]Olivia Barclay and *Horary Astrology Rediscovered.*

CHAPTER 9

Narcissistic Personality Disorder

THE USE OF THE TERM narcissism to effectively describe excessive vanity and self-centeredness predates by many years the modern medical classification of narcissistic personality disorder. The condition was named after a mythological Greek named Narcissus who became *infatuated* with his own reflection in a lake. He eventually died there because he could not tear himself away from the admiration of his image. The term narcissistic personality disorder was introduced by *Kemberg* in 1967 and narcissistic personality disorder was first proposed by *Heinz Kohut* in 1968.

Symptoms

The symptoms of narcissistic personality disorder are as follows: reacting strongly to criticism with anger, shame, or humiliation; taking advantage of others in order to attain goals; exaggeration, especially where self-importance, achievements, and talents are concerned; unrealistic fantasies toward success, beauty, power, intellect, and romance; requiring constant attention and positive reinforcement from others; easily becoming jealous; lacking empathy and disregarding the feelings of others; becoming obsessed and pursuing selfish goals; trouble maintaining healthy and prosperous relationships; becoming easily hurt and rejected; setting unrealistic goals; wanting the best of everything; and constantly appearing unemotional.

In addition to these symptoms, an individual may be prone to displaying dominance and arrogance with a strong inclination to demonstrate superiority and power. The symptoms of narcissistic personality disorder are very similar to the traits of individuals with self-esteem and confidence issues. Differentiation occurs when the underlying psychological structures of these traits are considered to be *pathological*. Narcissists have such an elevated sense of self-worth that they value themselves as inherently better than others. Yet they have extremely fragile levels of self-esteem and therefore cannot deal with criticism. Likewise, they will often try to compensate for this inner fragility by belittling or disparaging others in an attempt to validate their own self-worth. Consequently, it is this *sadistic* tendency that is characteristic of narcissism, as opposed to other psychological conditions that may be affecting their levels of self-worth.

Causes

The cause of this condition is relatively unknown; however, below is a list of possibilities:

- Oversensitive temperament at birth.
- Excessive admiration that is never balanced with realistic feedback.
- Excessive praise for good behaviors or alternatively excessive criticism for bad behaviors in childhood.
- Overindulgence and overvaluation by parents or peers.
- Being praised for perceived exceptional looks or abilities by adults.
- Severe emotional abuse in childhood.
- Unpredictable or unreliable care-giving from parents.
- Valued by parents as a means to regulate their own self-esteem or importance.

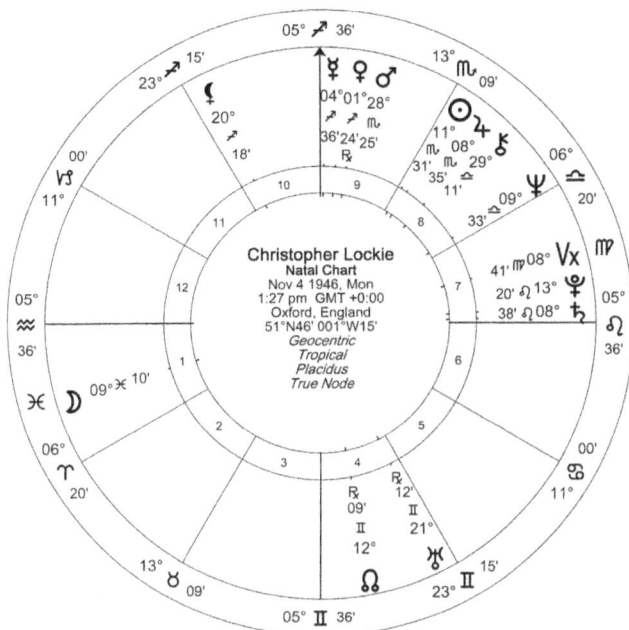

05° ♐ 36'

23° ♐ 15'

04°01°28'
☿ ♀ ♂
♐ ♐ ♏
36'24'25'
℞

13° ♏ 09'

☉ ♃
11° ♏ 08° ⚷
31' ♏ 29°
35'
11'

06° ♎ 20'

♆ 09° 33'

00' ♑ 11°

20° ♐ 18'

♈ 20°

♈ 15'

41' ♍ 08° Vx ♍
20' ♌ 13° ♇
38' ♌ 08° ♄

05° ♌ 36'

05° ♒ 36'

♓ ☽ 09° ♓ 10'

Christopher Lockie
Natal Chart
Nov 4 1946, Mon
1:27 pm GMT +0:00
Oxford, England
51°N46' 001°W15'
Geocentric
Tropical
Placidus
True Node

06° ♈ 20'

00' ♋ 11°

13° ♉ 09'

℞ 12'
♊ 21°
℞ 09'
♊ 12'

♅ 23° ♊ 15'

☊ 05° ♊ 36'

Astrological Diagnosis

Let us now evaluate this condition from an astrological perspective.[1]

Chris's chart emphasizes the presence of this unpredictable and all-too-common condition that is becoming more widespread in the world, especially throughout modern Western civilization. But aside from the proliferation of this now deemed "mental illness," levels of self-centeredness are approaching a crisis point, especially as we live in an age of illusion and glamor. But most concerning is the desire of the majority to emulate this celebrity image. Today there is too much emphasis placed on the physical body, especially in the name of glamor, but we possess little or no awareness of the stress that we are systematically incurring upon the physical body because of a sublime need to satisfy the external ego.

Most disturbing is our lack of understanding and the decomposition of the inherent yearning to reconnect with our spiritual self and with its divine capacity for evolutionary growth—spiritual meaning in the sense of our true identity. This lack of spiritual acceptance can in effect be a catalyst for the onset of illness, and it is often referred to by spiritual therapists as *self-denial*. Interestingly, narcissistic personality disorder is a condition that can *halt* spiritual growth and it can also have deleterious effects on the soul in the afterlife.[2]

Meanwhile, we can clearly see the emphasis of this condition in the chart from an interconnected planetary viewpoint. We can do this by first looking at one specific significator: the Nodes. They occupy Gemini and Sagittarius, the polarity of *sanity* verses *insanity*. We can see a cosmic catalyst emerging that is an almost certain starting point for the onset of this mentally-orientated illness.

According to author Louise Hay, narcissistic personality disorder occurs because of "a *refusal* to deal with the world as it is." In accordance with this affirmation, the rulers of the Nodes (Mercury and Jupiter) are positioned in the particular zones of the chart where the refusal to deal with the world as it is becomes all too evident. This is the eighth and ninth houses, which are the houses of dominance, power, and of the inflated ego. Mercury is conjunct the Midheaven in the South Nodal sign of Sagittarius (detriment). In addition, Gemini and Sagittarius rule the fourth-tenth house polarity. The Moon's square to Mercury is conjunct the Midheaven and its inconjunction to Saturn is part of a Yod configuration with Neptune from the Sun and Chiron-ruled seventh house; this means this condition has been carried over from a past life or lives.

However, the Yod, commonly referred to as the finger of God, is traditionally pointing the way toward spiritual upliftment and personal change. This is further emphasized by the first house and the Neptune-ruled Pisces Moon. Maybe personal change wasn't achieved in a past life, as the all-knowing Sagittarius South Node can often bolster narrow-mindedness coupled by a refusal to assimilate advice and potential life-changing information. Therefore, a Sagittarius South Node has the tendency to believe that it doesn't need anyone because it can achieve everything by itself and of its own egotistical viewpoint, which was no doubt a prevalent Sagittarius concept that the soul adopted throughout a past life or lives. Moreover, the Sagittarius South Node sees no need or practical purpose for such measures as rationality, constructive reasoning, or necessary interaction, especially with those it considers as not on its wavelength.

This lack of understanding is further necessitated by the Sun's separating conjunction to Jupiter from the eighth house of inheritances and its applied inconjunction (a need for necessary adjustment) to the Nodes, coupled by the Moon's square to the Nodes, which is also in an applied aspect. The Moon's square to the Nodes can indicate a breakdown in communication (Gemini-Mercury) during the individual's upbringing between the parents, as the Nodes are posited in the fourth and tenth houses, symbolizing both the mother and the father. Alternatively, the Moon's square can also indicate a communication breakdown of some description in a past life because the tenth is ruled traditionally by Saturn.

Jupiter also links into the Nodes with a bi-quintile, to Neptune with an applied trine, and to Pluto with a separating sextile. Interestingly, the Nodes rule the throat chakra with Gemini ruling the nervous system and Sagittarius ruling the pituitary gland. The pituitary gland is a small ductless gland located at the base of the spine that secretes the various hormones that are essential for growth and other bodily functions. This important gland is, in effect, overseen by the throat chakra.

Putting all these causes of narcissistic personality disorder aside for a moment, another significator or catalyst marking the cause of this condition is hormonal imbalance because there always has to be a physical trigger for every illness, mental or otherwise. Jupiter's square to the Ascendant, Saturn, and Pluto would seem to corroborate this, along with Mercury's square to the Moon and its conjunction to Venus, which are linked to the Sun (Leo) and the seventh house.

With the Sun, Mercury, Venus, and Jupiter all *elevated* on the oriental side of the chart we could almost assume that these planets are indeed looking across toward the eastern side. It's almost as if the Ascendant side represents a reflection of the abounding ego that proliferates via this condition, similar to narcissus who became *obsessed* with his own reflection, and thus the crux of narcissistic personality disorder.

Another factor that needs to be considered here is Mars, which is opposed to the fixed star Algol from the third to the ninth house. Is Algol currently at 25 degrees of Taurus creating that reflective illusion (2+5 = 7 Neptune), especially as its position lies very close to the IC? Or maybe Algol's presence in the third house has and continues to disrupt those personal environmental issues? As Algol (cruelty) occupies Taurus, the sign of stability, *instability* was a profound issue in childhood and it continues to be so. Furthermore, I am aware that Chris was sent to a boarding school as a young boy, with boarding schools being linked to that third-ninth house polarity. I can also confirm that Chris was abused at age eight. This childhood tragedy and trauma effect (the Nodes) could have acted as a further trigger for the intensifying effects of narcissistic personality disorder.

Finally, with the North Node signifying future direction, the chart suggests that this condition is a karmically-ingrained and integral part of that all-important future direction.

Prognosis

So, what can we deduce from all of this planetary activity? Without doubt I believe that the seeds of this illness were set in a previous life or possibly within many lifetimes. If we adopt author Ivy Goldstein-Jacobson's hypothesis that the Nodes are responsible for bringing *trauma* and *tragedy* into our lives, then clearly the Gemini-Sagittarius polarity has had a profound influence on the chart with Gemini ruling the fourth and Sagittarius ruling the tenth in a square with the Moon and with the Moon as the apex of the Yod. This configuration has brought trauma throughout the early stages of life, which then transmuted into tragedy in later life as the Sun's connection to the seventh brought alienation and stagnation—another likely probability of this unyielding disease.

Chris has suffered from this condition most of his life, and like every form of illness and disease it has been subject to ebbs and flows, especially during those intermittent periods when the intellectual, emotional, and mastery biorhythms were low. However, since the latter part of 2005, the condition had gradually managed to get a more consistent foothold so to speak, hence it has started to overwhelm him. One trigger was, I believe, transiting Uranus conjoining his natal Moon from the first house of the self, the effects of this transit further extenuated the effects of the Yod. Uranus is widely associated with mental illness and trauma in a particular field, and because this planet is the polarity influence of the Sun and Leo, self-importance can be a prominent issue that has become stigmatised throughout the many self-relevant forms of mental illness.

In 2007, Uranus was square the Nodes. In addition, the transiting Nodes were square his natal Nodes, creating a *déjà vu* effect in the psyche. As a result the psychological memories of mental and physical abuse surfaced from childhood and past lives, causing a further deterioration in Chris's condition. In effect Chris descended further into the transfixed realm of *self-denial*.

Conclusion

Unfortunately, Chris continually struggles to understand the nature and the self-inflicted consequences associated with this illness. Therefore, he is in a state of constant denial whereby he quickly closes down once he is forced to confront the symptoms of this self-induced condition. Because of the stringent planetary complexities in his chart he has found it difficult to embrace change. He continues to participaste in regular therapy and healing sessions and in addition he frequently visits astrologers, all of which have proven to be *ineffective*, partly because he is looking for a quick fix. Until Chris grasps the dynamics of this illness he will continue to suffer from it.

Unfortunately, if levels of self-centerdness continue to foster narcissistic personality disorder, it will become a serious global concern. In retrospect I would estimate that this illness will become the king of all mental health issues within a decade.

Endnotes

[1] Information courtesy of the *Medical Journal of Health and Well Being* published by Collins.

[2] Research has suggested that all forms of mental illness have a profound impact on the soul after death especially narcissistic personality disorder. Because the soul has been so heavily traumatised by paranoia, conflict and psychological abuse (the crux of all mental illness), it will invariably be in denial thus refusing to acknowledge that the death of the physical body has actually taken place; therefore it will often refuse to leave the refuge of its known and safe environment, hence the physical home.

CHAPTER 10

Cardiovascular and Lung Disease

CARDIOVASCULAR DISEASE IS A CLASS of diseases that involve the heart or blood vessels. It refers to any disease that affects the cardiovascular system such as cardiac disease, vascular diseases of the brain and kidneys, and peripheral arterial diseases. The causes of cardiovascular disease are diverse but *atherosclerosis* and *hypertension* are the most common. Additionally, with aging comes a number of physiological and morphological changes that alter cardiovascular function and thus lead to increased risk of cardiovascular diseases, even in healthy asymptomatic individuals.

Cardiovascular disease is the leading cause of death worldwide, although since the 1970s, mortality rates have declined throughout many high-income countries. However, at the same time, cardiovascular death and disease have increased at a fast rate in low- and middle-income countries. Although cardiovascular disease usually affects older adults, the antecedents of cardiovascular disease, notably atherosclerosis, begin in early life, making primary prevention efforts necessary from childhood. There is therefore increased emphasis on preventing atherosclerosis by modifying certain risk factors such as healthy eating, exercise, and the avoidance of smoking.[1]

Angela was diagnosed with narrowing of the arteries and an enlarged left ventricle, which had ceased functioning; the ventricles are responsible for the heart's pumping action. A weakened heart with only one functioning ventricle will find it increasingly difficult to function to full capacity. In effect, the heart cannot operate at maximum efficiency with only one functioning ventricle, and consequently this will cause a malfunction in the body's immune system. A malfunctioning immune system will have detrimental effects on other organs, such as suppressed lung function.

In addition, Angela had suffered from a stroke, which initially left her paralyzed on the left side of her body (the afflicted ventricle side). This corresponds to her planets being posited mostly on the eastern (left) side of the chart, indicating a debilitating weakness in this area. Since the initial diagnosis she had two stents inserted, and she also suffers from Type 2 diabetes, which has mainly been caused by the daily ingesting of steroids. Her kidneys are also in the early stages of renal failure, initially caused by the large amounts of prescription drugs, especially the high dosage of water tablets she is having to take as a result of the extensive heart problem. As indicated in the birth chart, this condition is genetically inherent as well as self-induced.

But before we examine her chart, she is dealing with another serious disease that is the direct result of her organs fighting against each other: pulmonary fibrosis.

Lung Disease: Pulmonary Fibrosis

Pulmonary fibrosis is the formation or development of excess fibrous connective tissue (fibrosis) in the lungs and therefore it is sometimes referred to as *honeycombing of the lungs*. Moreover, pulmonary fibrosis occurs because of scarring of the lung tissue that can be the result of other lung-related diseases as well as exposure to asbestos, coal dust, spoors emitted from the feathers of tropical birds, or exposure to damp environments. Symptoms of pulmonary fibrosis can vary from case to case but are mainly confined to the following category: shortness of breath, particularly with exertion. Chronic coughing and sometimes fine inspiratory crackles can be heard at the lung bases on auscultation. Fatigue coupled with a general feeling of weakness are also symptoms of pulmonary fibrosis, as is chest discomfort and a loss of appetite. In some cases there is rapid weight loss or gain.

Angela contracted this illness as a direct result of her heart condition and in addition from the long-term inhalation of mould spoors that are commonly associated with a damp environment, a factor that caused scarring of the lung. She has lived in this environment for more than twenty years. She also has alveolitis (inflammation of the alveoli) because of her weakened lung capacity.

Astrological Diagnosis

We can see from her chart that there are many significators that emphasize the proliferation effect of these detrimental diseases, most notably being the Moon in an applied inconjunction to Uranus, which is conjunct the Leo Midheaven (heart) with the Sun ruling the ninth and tenth houses symbolizing the arterial system and potential remedies, medical or otherwise. The Sun is *disposed* (Virgo) in the eleventh house, ruling the heart's circulation and the oxidation of the blood. The Moon's sign of Cancer also rules the ninth with a very small percentage ruling the eighth house (the house of death, inheritances, and lingering illness).

The Moon also connects to Jupiter with a separating square and with an applied semi-square to Saturn. Jupiter is the accidental ruler of Saturn's rulership house (the second) and Saturn rules the Moon's rulership house (the third). Saturn's declination is eight degrees south, and eight degrees of any sign signifies accidents and tragedy because tragedy is emphasized by the Nodes. The ruler of the South Node (Venus) occupies the twelfth house

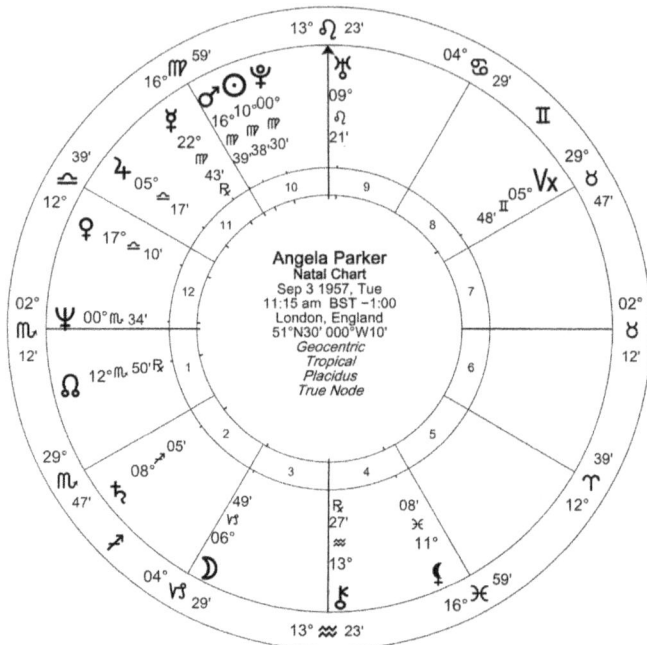

Angela Parker
Natal Chart
Sep 3 1957, Tue
11:15 am BST –1:00
London, England
51°N30' 000°W10'
Geocentric
Tropical
Placidus
True Node

and is largely unaspected, especially by major aspects, whereas the ruler of the North Node, Pluto, occupies the tenth house (Saturn) in Virgo at zero degrees (symbolizing a fear of the unknown) and is semi-square the exalted Venus.

Neptune, the traditional ruler of the twelfth house, rises on the Ascendant and is exactly conjunct the first house cusp and rules the fourth and fifth houses (the fifth rules the heart), perhaps indicating a genetic weakness. The Nodes are also square Uranus and the Midheaven from the first and seventh houses. Chiron is conjunct the IC (crown chakra) and opposes Uranus. Gemini, which rules the lungs is the primary ruler of the eighth house, and Libra, which rules the kidneys, rules the twelfth house of hospitals. As indicated earlier, Angela's planets are mainly posited in the eastern half of the chart, representing the left side of the body, which comes under the rulership of Cancer. Cancer's ruling planet is the Moon, which is clearly the catalyst for the onset of these illnesses to which the seeds were set in childhood. The Moon opposes the Part of Fortune, which is in close conjunction to the ninth house cusp[2], and also in detriment.

We can determine from this information that the cardiovascular and lung disease with the inclusion of kidney failure are inherent karmic conditions. Cardiovascular disease is a condition that was clearly evident within the generational family unit. Maybe the soul came back this time in an attempt to better understand the dynamics of these conditions that it may have overlooked, and to dispose of them? With Pluto's connection to the Nodes it is my belief that there is unfinished business to take care of, especially of a genetic nature. This hypothesis could be further necessitated by Mercury's retrograde position in the eleventh house at 22 Virgo with Virgo's modern ruler, Chiron, also retrograde in the fourth house of foundations, with twenty-two degrees symbolizing new beginnings and representing *signposts* along the innate journey of life.[3] The stellium of planets in Virgo is likely to be a further significator of this possibility; however, with all that analytical Virgo influencing the tenth and eleventh houses linked to Uranus via a semi-square and semi-sextile from the eastern half of the chart, Angela will take some convincing.

Metaphorically speaking, Angela suffers from a broken heart. This seems evident because the Leo-ruled Midheaven (the heart chakra) has been besieged by Uranus (fragmentation) and is linked to Black Moon Lilith via an inconjunction from the fourth house in deception-oriented Pisces with Uranus being in detriment. When we determine the position of the South Node from the seventh house in Taurus, which is potentially ruled by Black Moon Lilith, we see a karmic connection unfolding. Taurus, which rules the root chakra, encompasses the entire seventh house; furthermore, its planetary ruler, Venus, sits in the Pisces-ruled twelfth house of karmic symbolism and incarceration, which is directly linked to the shadow side of Black Moon Lilith. So this brings up an important question: was Angela deceived or was she in fact the deceiver?

It is reasonable to hypothesize that in past lives she was psychologically abused in some way (Scorpio North Node) by lovers, marital partners, and business associates. The trauma, as symbolized by the South Node, has deeply affected her heart as indicated by its square to Uranus and the Midheaven, which is further indicated by the Sun's square to Saturn from the Saturn-ruled tenth house to the Venus-ruled second house. Algol's position from the seventh doesn't really help matters as this dark star's influence disposes the seventh house and all that it stands for—perhaps a certain malign influence is dominantly present? With the North Node's position in the first house (the sacral chakra) it is clear that she must learn to *heal* herself and take ultimate control over her life (Scorpio).

The heart, lung, and kidney failings were diagnosed during a period of extreme biorhythm depletion and heavy planetary transits involving the three outer planets all debilitated by squares, inconjunctions, semi-squares, and oppositions.

Prognosis

The Nodes can definitely be looked upon as a clear-cut primary health disposition of this chart, partly because they are posited in important and significant health-oriented houses. Conceptually, the Nodes represent a dichotomy of ideals, meaning they represent the polarity of ultimate potential or distress. Because of the position of the Nodes in the chart (first-seventh houses) Angela is continually torn in her feelings. Does she do what's best for her or does she put others first? Having Venus as the ruler of the South Node sign in her twelfth house draws her toward matters of personalized guilt, and she tends to feel sorry for those less fortunate souls, especially those whose unfortunate predicament is a representation of their own volition.

Interestingly, it is this negative emotion of guilt that has been the psychological backdrop for the onset of illness. In effect her own psychological mistreatment in a past life now causes her to rigorously defend (Scorpio) those souls facing a similar disposition. But realistically, she must *invest* those South Node energies into strengthening (Taurus) her somewhat lost and traumatized psyche indicated by the Scorpio first house North Node in order to move on and use her wealth of Scorpio related talents.

Another factor to take into consideration is that Angela frequently becomes debilitated by cellulites ("buried anger and self-punishment," according to author Louise Hay). Cellulites or *cellulite build up* is a form of blood poisoning, and the indication of this complaint could be Saturn's position at 8 Sagittarius; Jupiter, ruler of Sagittarius, rules blood. Eight degrees of Sagittarius is an Azimene Degree (AD), which according to author Ivy Goldstein Jacobson are "deficient degrees that can point to a debilitating condition in the body—a disability, a wound or a flaw in a certain part of the body, etc.," especially when they are in conjunction to the Ascendant or the Ascendant ruler.[4]

Saturn is posited in the second house (representing the root chakra hence lower legs and ankles) and is opposite the eighth of toxicity and inflammation; the eighth house is the traditional rulership house of Mars. As we have already determined, Saturn is square the Sun. Saturn is intercepted in the second with its ruler, Aquarius (lower legs and ankles), ruling the third and fourth, symbolizing the life force energy and digestion. Pisces (Neptune and poisoning) is also on the fourth. Chiron, the modern ruler of Virgo (Sun sign), is closely conjunct the IC.

Gout (self-punishment) is also a disease that can invariably be linked to cellulites, and is often triggered by a combination of poor digestion (fourth house) and a love of rich food (second house); in this chart, Mars and Venus rule the sixth house of diet. In addition, gout can be triggered by exceptionally high levels of urate in the body (eighth house), a condition from which Angela frequently suffers. In my estimation there is strong enough evidence to suggest that Saturn in an Azimene degree *is* in fact the primary catalyst for the onset of reccurring cellulites.

Interestingly, the rulers of the Nodes feature once more in this medical equation because they rule the sixth house of health opposing the twelfth and Neptune.

Conclusion

This has been a difficult chart to work with; however, there is much potential buried within its psychologically-orientated matrix. But to Angela, *potential* is an alien concept because it has frequently been hidden from view because of Neptune's extremely close proximity to the Ascendant. Essentially, Angela has been enveloped by a fog of self-sacrifice and self-deceit, which pertains to a complete lack of direction. Moreover, Angela has been offset by a misguided form of guilt called self-induced delusion. However, in this case the self-induced delusion factor systematically draws heavily on the purse strings of the welfare state (Neptune symbolizing the beggar), meaning that she has become a long-term prisoner (Neptune twelfth house) trapped in the institutionalised entrapment of the social welfare system, where often there can be no escape. In order for her health to improve and for her to extend her lifespan she must relinquish the curse-ridden guilt that she carries daily on her shoulders (Saturn in the second opposing a Gemini ruled eighth house) and find her own personalized niche in life by believing in herself.

Endnotes

[1]Information courtesy of the *Medical Encyclopaedia of Health and Well Being* published by Collins.

[2]For a precise account of the Part of Fortune I recommend reading *The Fortunes of Astrology*.

[3]Olivia Barclay with her excellent book *Horary Astrology Rediscovered*.

[4]Azimene degrees are: 6, 7, 8, 9, and 10 Taurus; 9, 10, 11, 12, 13, 14, and 15 Cancer; 18, 27, and 28 Leo; 19 and 28 Scorpio; 1, 7, 8, 18, and 19 Sagittarius; 26, 27, 28, and 29 Capricorn; and 18 and 19 Aquarius.

CHAPTER 11

Narcolepsy

NARCOLEPSY IS A CHRONIC NEUROLOGICAL disorder caused initially by the brain's inability to regulate sleep-wake cycles. People who suffer from narcolepsy usually experience disturbed nocturnal sleep and an abnormal daytime sleep pattern that can often be confused with insomnia. When falling asleep, narcoleptics generally experience the REM stage of sleep within five minutes, while most people do not experience REM sleep until an hour or so later.

Although narcolepsy is *not* caused by mental illness or psychological problems, it can be associated with psychological patterns and memories within the brain. It is most likely related to a number of genetic mutations and abnormalities that affect specific biological factors in the brain, combined with an environmental trigger during the brain's development, such as a virus.

The term narcolepsy derives from the French word *narcolepsie* meaning "attack" or "seizure."

Symptoms

The main characteristic of narcolepsy is *Excessive Daytime Sleepiness* (EDS), which occurs even after an adequate nighttime sleep. A person with narcolepsy is likely to become drowsy or fall asleep or just be very tired during the day and often at inappropriate times and places. Daytime naps may occur with little or no warning and may prove to be irresistible, and *napping* can occur several times a day. Daytime naps are typically refreshing, but their effects only last a few hours. Drowsiness may also persist for prolonged periods of time. In addition, nighttime sleep may become fragmented with frequent awakenings. Common narcolepsy symptoms include:

- Cataplexy (loss of muscle control). Often, narcolepsy may cause sudden loss of muscle control whilst awake, usually triggered by powerful emotions, such as laughing or crying.

- Hallucinations. Some people with narcolepsy experience vivid, sometimes frightening, visual and auditory sensations while falling asleep or upon awakening.

- Sleep Paralysis. Some people are unable to move or talk at the beginning or end of sleep.

- Microsleep. This typifies a brief sleep pattern during which the body continues to function (e.g. talking, doing daily chores etc), and then to awaken with no memory of the activities.

- Night Wakefulness. Experiencing wakefulness at night means periods of hot flashes, elevated heart rate, and intense alertness.[1]

Causes

While researchers continue to seek the root cause of narcolepsy, the general consensus is that it is genetic, accompanied by an environmental trigger that affects the chemical makeup of the brain. Scientists have discovered that people with narcolepsy are deficient of *hypocretin* (also called orexin), a chemical in the brain that activates arousal and regulates sleep. Narcoleptics generally do not have as many Hcrt cells (neurons that secrete hypocretin), inhibiting the ability to control alertness, which accounts for the tendency to fall asleep. Scientists are now working to develop a treatment that will supplement hypocretin levels in order to reduce the symptoms of narcolepsy.

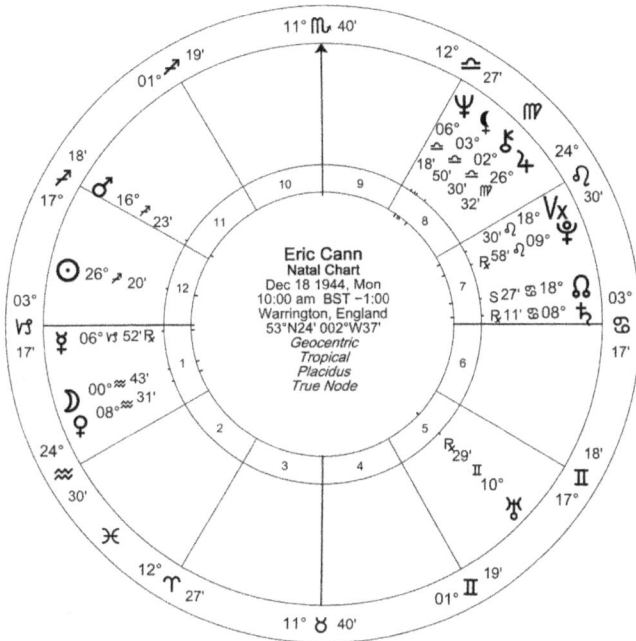

Eric Cann
Natal Chart
Dec 18 1944, Mon
10:00 am BST −1:00
Warrington, England
53"N24' 002"W37'
Geocentric
Tropical
Placidus
True Node

Astrological Diagnosis

Asatrologer Cathie Gill comments in an article that was published in July 2009 *Astrology and Medicine* newsletter: "although the cause of narcolepsy is unknown, it appears that there is a genetic factor involved."

There is much emphasis on Saturn in Eric's chart. Saturn is the chart ruler and the ruler of the South Node's sign, Capricorn, and dominates the entire first house cusp with its co-sign Aquarius. Saturn also co-rules the third eye chakra along with Pisces-Neptune (sleep and the dream state). The Sun is in the twelfth house of sleep and partly rules the seventh (Saturn's accidental domain). With the Sun's square to Jupiter, the ruler of the Sun sign, and with Jupiter debilitated in Virgo in the eighth house it is possible that Eric was *incarcerated* or *imprisoned* in previous lives, whereby he was unable to attain reasonable amounts of sleep and thus was subjected to sleep deprivation. A course of Deep Memory Process regression therapy confirmed these past life findings.[2]

Narcolepsy maybe the brain's way of slowing the body down, which then allows the life force energy to catch up on all of those sleepless nights that are deeply indented with a karmic signature.

The ruler of the North Node's sign, the Moon, is also connected to Saturn because it is in Saturn's traditional sign of Aquarius. Mercury in Capricorn is rising and forms an exact square to Neptune, Neptune is square Saturn, and Saturn opposes Mercury, forming a t-square. The Sun is connected to the t-square via a sesquiquadrate to Pluto in the Sun's sign of Leo (the genetic factor transmitted via the interconnected heart). This t-square formation is the catalyst for narcolepsy.

According to author Louise Hay, "narcolepsy is caused by extreme fear, coupled by an inability to cope, and a need to get away from it all." Eric's chart illustrates the concept of getting away from it all, possibly a psychological reflection of those strenuous past life events that he wants to escape. Essentially, this is what I would refer to as an "inherent closing down or switching off chart." An accurate hypothesis would be to indicate that narcolepsy was inherited from the father, which is denoted in part by Saturn and the South Node in Capricorn. This probable theory is consolidated by Saturn's connection to genetic-oriented Pluto via an applied semi-sextile. Deep Memory Process also revealed that Eric was imprisoned on several occasions with his current life father—the genetic connection.

However, the physical catalyst for narcolepsy was set in motion when Eric was about age eight and he contracted a life-threatening virus of an unknown kind and origin (Pluto rules viruses). Satur is at 8 Cancer in the t-square configuration and eight degrees signifies accidents and trauma; eight also represents Eric's age when this crisis occurred. For Eric, trauma (the Nodes), occurred in childhood because Saturn disposes of the

Moon's sign, Cancer. Eric's body became intoxicated by poison (Neptune), some of which were deposited in the brain. Consequently, he was in a coma for eight days. The surgeons eventually drained off the poison but they insisted it would in time (Saturn) have deleterious effects on the body. Eric did recover from his ordeal, but narcolepsy began to occur around age twenty five at about the time when transiting Neptune conjoined his Midheaven.

Eight is a reccurring theme in his chart with the stellium of planets in his eighth house and Saturn's inconjunction to Venus at 8 Aquarius. Number eight is ruled by Uranus, and Uranus rules despots and dictators. The position of Uranus in Eric's chart (fifth house) may be a further indication that his soul was somehow suppressed and subjugated in a past life.

In addition, I have noticed that his narcolepsy intensifies during periods of biorhythm depletion, especially when the physical, emotional, intellectual, and aesthetic rhythms are below the midline and at the transition of *critical*. During such a time of biorhythm depletion Eric fell asleep behind the wheel of his car while driving through a town's busy shopping area; fortunately there were no altercations or injuries. Narcolepsy is said to be activated when there is a sudden build-up of responsibilities imposing upon the body from external sources, and becomes too much for the brain to endure. Where Eric is concerned this certainly appears to have been the case.

Maybe Eric had also asked in an intuitive way to be taken from the world for a limited time, in which case he has spent many reflective hours in the confines of a Neptunian hospital bed (twelfth house Sun). This would have resulted in Eric being nurtured and cared for (Cancer North Node seventh house). Responsibility may have been removed for a time (Saturn's debilitation in Cancer) in order for him to contemplate (Pluto). Coupled with these bouts of being cared for and the frequent episodes of narcolepsy, this is a chart that most definitely symbolizes the switching off factor. Also, it is fair to say that Eric needs plenty of TLC in order to heal from his past life experiences, which is validated by his chart.

Prognosis

Narcolepsy is still regarded as a mysterious, intrusive disease for which there is no known cure. All viruses have a physiological and psychological connection that points to an imbalance in the life force energy, or alternatively to some form of unfinished business, which falls under the contemplative jurisdiction of Pluto. Eric's first-seventh house polarity, which is co-ruled by Saturn, Sun, and Moon, seems to hold the key to this deep-set affliction, and these planets rule the crown, heart, and third eye chakra (pineal gland), the center of psychic response indicating powerful past life memories and trauma.

Interestingly, the pineal gland, a reddish body in the posterior position of the skull cavity and somewhat of an enigma to many astrologers, falls under the rulership of both Neptune and Uranus. It is believed that narcolepsy (caused by a potential virus that is born from the effects of continual sleep deprivation) can prevent the pineal gland from being activated, rendering all memories *inactive*. Looking at the geometric closeness of the t-square in Eric's chart with Neptune at the apex of the t-square would certainly validate this theory. The elevated position of Neptune (chemicals) and its exact square to Mercury from the first house could also be responsible for the lack of hypocretin in the brain. From this position Neptune would *deceive* the body into believing that there are adequate supplies of this chemical in the body. Inadequate supplies of hypocretin would most likely be responsible for causing a malfunction in the body's internal clock (Saturn and its square to Neptune), causing the body to shut down at any given time (hence the onset of narcolepsy). This is further vindicated by the Saturn-Neptune square.

Inevitably, Saturn would suppress Mercury's brain activity

and Neptune would render the body *neutral*, placing it in the unconscious sleep state. But because of the involvement of Saturn the sleep state would only occur for a limited time. Uranus (also connected with brain activity) is in Mercury's sign of Gemini, and has been deemed by some astrologers as the *awakener*, and would therefore act as the body's alarm clock. During my experiments with Eric his frequent narcoleptic napping lasted mostly for a duration that rarely exceeded eight minutes (Saturn's natal degree). Neptune's elevated position at the top of the chart can be likened to that of the snooze button on the Uranus-ruled alarm clock.

Furthermore, it could be said that Saturn is on the brink of further debilitation as its natal degree is only forty-nine minutes away from 9 Cancer, which is an Azimene degree. This would almost certainly confirm that the narcolepsy, operating as a connected psychological element, would reverberate as a psychological echo or a physical flaw that manifests from the karmic vaults of those long forgotten times in our distant past.

I am not suggesting that this particular prognosis is the same for every narcoleptic sufferer. On the contrary what I am pointing out is that the genetic physical implications of this disease are greatly relevant to each individual case.

Conclusion

Eric is still undergoing DMP therapy and is also receiving vibrational healing therapy to cleanse his chakras. As a result of this past life release and holistic cleansing, Eric's napping has become less frequent, especially when he is out and about. Although Eric will continue to suffer from this illness, he will acquire a better understanding of it and therefore will be able to retake control of his life.

Endnotes
[1]Information courtesy of Wikipedia.

²Regression therapy is often used as a way of unfolding events and unlocking trauma that has incurred throughout previous incarnations. Likewise this powerful technique can be the crucial foundation and the basis for the ancient symbolic system of practice known as evolutionary astrology. These past life techniques and astrological systems are beautifully explained in Patricia L. Walsh's book: *Understanding Karmic Complexes*, published by the Wessex Astrologer. In addition, for more information about DMP (Deep Memory Process) refer to the teachings of Roger Woolger.

CHAPTER 12

Alcohol Abuse

ALCOHOLISM IS A BROAD TERM. In general, alcoholism means the compulsive and uncontrolled consumption of alcoholic beverages, which is usually to the detriment of the drinker's health, personal relationships, and social standing. Today, alcoholism is considered a disease or an addictive illness.

The biological mechanisms that cause alcoholism are not clearly understood. Social environment, stress, mental health, family history, age, ethnic group, and gender all influence the risks that can develop into this condition. Alcohol abuse has the potential to damage almost every organ in the body, including the brain. The cumulative toxic effects of chronic alcohol abuse can cause both medical and psychiatric problems.

Symptoms

Long-term alcohol abuse can cause a number of physical symptoms, including cirrhosis of the liver, pancreatitis, epilepsy, polyneuropathy, alcoholic dementia, heart disease, nutritional deficiencies, peptic ulcers, and sexual dysfunction, and can eventually be *fatal*. Other physical effects include cardiovascular disease, malabsorbtion, alcoholic liver disease, and cancer. Damage to the central nervous system and peripheral nervous system can also occur from sustained alcohol consumption. In addition, a wide range of immunologic defects can result and there may be a generalized skeletal fragility leading to accidental injury and resulting in a propensity for bone fractures.

Causes

A complex mixture of genetic and environmental factors influences the risk of the development of alcoholism. Genes that influence the metabolism of alcohol also influence the risk of alcoholism and therefore may be indicated by a family history of alcoholism. Research has discovered that alcohol use at an early age may influence the expression of the genes, which increases the risk of alcohol dependence. Individuals who have a genetic disposition to alcoholism are also more likely to begin drinking at an earlier age.

Also, at a younger age the onset of drinking is associated with an increased risk to the development of alcoholism, and it is a fact that about forty percent of alcoholics will drink *excessively* by their late adolescence. It is not entirely known whether this association is causal, and some researchers have been known to disagree with this viewpoint. A high testosterone concentration during pregnancy may also be a risk factor for the later development of alcohol dependence.

Severe childhood trauma is also associated with a general increase in the risk of alcohol dependency. Lack of peer or family support is widely associated with an increased risk of alcoholism. Genetics and adolescence are associated with an increased sensitivity to the neurotoxic effects of chronic alcohol abuse. Cortical degeneration due to the neurotoxic effects increases impulsive behavior, which may contribute to the development, persistence, and severity of alcohol use disorders. There is evidence that with abstinence there is a reversal of at least some of the alcohol-induced central nervous system damage.[1]

Astrological Diagnosis

Again we turn our attention to the sign rulers of the Nodes and their position and influence in the natal chart. On closer inspection we see the Nodes residing at 22 Scorpio-Taurus from the second-eighth house polarity. Peter's alcohol abuse began in

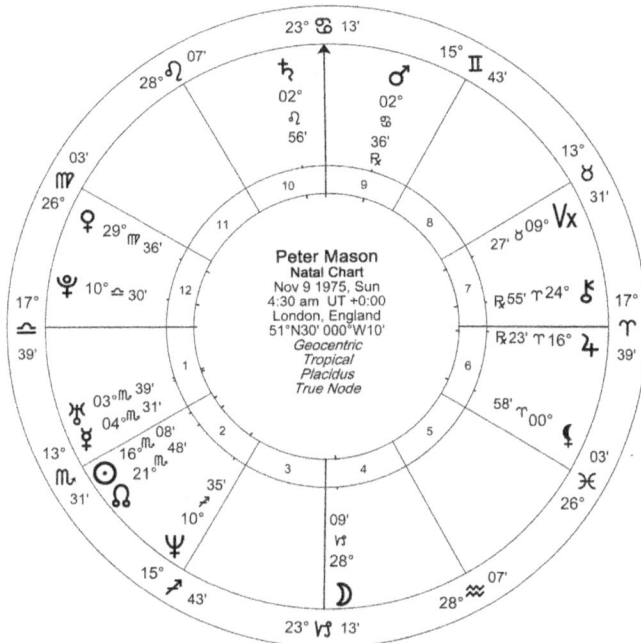

Peter Mason
Natal Chart
Nov 9 1975, Sun
4:30 am UT +0:00
London, England
51°N30' 000°W10'
Geocentric
Tropical
Placidus
True Node

early life, around age fourteen (1+4 = 5, Peter's life path number), and even then his alcoholism was publicly known (twenty-two degrees). This caused turmoil and heartache for his parents and others who were close to him.

What defines Peter's chart is the condition of the Moon, which is debilitated in Capricorn and at 28 Capricorn, an Azimene Degree indicating an emotional disposition or flaw within his personality. Peter does have a problem expressing his emotions, and although this is not necessarily a major problem in the physical sense, it does nonetheless indicate a psychological tendency because the Moon is tied into a t-square with Mercury and Uranus at the apex (Uranus is exalted in Scorpio). These are thus the planets that clearly define our psychological and emotional parameters in life. The Moon opposes Saturn from the Sun's sign of Leo, which can indicate the profound effects of an inconjunction as the signs are incomparable; the natal Sun conjoins the North Node and opposes the South Node.

The rulers of the Nodal signs, Venus and Pluto, reside in the twelfth house with Pluto receiving a sextile from Neptune. Pluto is traditionally debilitated in Libra so essentially it has become *overpowered* by Venus and possibly Black Moon Lilith, which resides in the tenth. Venus in its fall receives a square from a debilitated Mars in Cancer from the ninth and nudges the Moon with a close orb trine. The ruler of the ninth, Jupiter, sits in Mars's rulership sign and opposes Pluto and the Ascendant. The fixed star *Algol* occupying the Pluto-Scorpio ruled eighth house of lingering illness and disease will significantly influence the Nodes and their ruling planets from this domain.

Interestingly, continual alcohol abuse has clearly affected Peter's sexual ability and capabilities. This can be clearly noted with the rulers of the Nodes tied in to the particular chakras that denote sexual performance: the root and the sacral. Mars (the sex drive), with its debilitation in Cancer, affects the natural role of the chakras, so in effect Mars's fall in Cancer has a significant draining effect on the energy emitted by the chakras. Furthermore, the energy of the affected chakras has somehow become crystallized, thereby creating calcification in the arteries of the heart, which was implemented by a disposed Saturn conjunct the Part of Fortune in the Sun's sign of Leo. Furthermore, the Sun conjoins Venus (the act of sexual intercourse) by way of a semi-square. In a way alcohol does have a *calcifying* effect on all the organs and it is this calcifying (hardening) effect that systematically destroys the organs.

Another primary concern, and one that has played a vital role in the onset of alcoholism, is Peter's inability to express himself in a clear and defined way. The culprit is of course *foggy* Neptune sitting in the Venus-ruled second house in Sagittarius close to the third house cusp of communication; Sagittarius rules the throat chakra and the throat chakra determines *self-expression*. In retrospect, he has a tendency to whisper in soliloquies and

Alcohol Abuse

monologues. Neptune's connection to the Nodes is clearly-defined and precise with its *exact* sextile to Pluto, ruler of the North Node's sign. Pluto is also rising in Neptune's twelfth house of escapism and personal inhibition, further enhancing his tendency to whisper in soliloquies and monologues. Essentially, Peter feels he is not being heard.

This is a very complex chart with many dignities and intricately tight orbs. Peter has had little or no choice when it comes to either dealing with the ongoing and self-destructive issue of alcoholism or to be completely enveloped by the sheer potency of Neptune's influence. Typically significant of Peter's alcohol abuse is the *trauma* that has been created, especially within his family unit. The family scenario of trauma plays out through the Moon and Saturn configuration, drawing the Nodes in from the second and eighth houses, the domains that represent trauma and tragedy. Consequently, if his alcoholism is not contained, *tragedy* will no doubt occur, especially once Neptune transits his sixth house of acute health problems.

For Peter the *alcoholism* symbolizes unfinished business (Pluto twelfth house and South Node in the eighth), and if it is not dealt with Peter could suffer from the onset of chronic kidney failure (Venus, Virgo, the solar plexus and the twelfth house of chronic health problems) just as he did in a past life as revealed under regression.

Interestingly, Peter's drinking intensifies during periods of emotional and spiritual biorhythm depletion, to which he often intimates that he feels totally rejected by life and its greater more meaningful cause, placing Peter's religious beliefs under the divine ethereal spotlight (Jupiter opposition the Ascendant).

Prognosis

According to author Louise Hay, "there are many significators associated with alcoholism, including a feeling of futility, guilt, inadequacy, and self-rejection."

Peter has suffered significantly from a lifetime of alcohol abuse. The sign rulers of the Nodes and their matriarchal connection to Neptune highlight this potentially debilitating condition. Another possible indicator for subsequent alcohol abuse is Venus's position in the twelfth house at 29 Virgo. Not only is Venus debilitated (in its fall) but twenty-nine degrees is effectively a degree of extreme uncertainty. Twenty nine degrees of any sign is said to be a "crossing the threshold" degree. As with all the natal positions of planets, Venus maintains its static position and so it borders at the inception of change. The effect of this planetary *uncertainty* will be particularly strong during Venus returns wherein the planet of harmony ventures into the unchartered territory of a new sign and in a zone that is said to bolster isolation, self-undoing, and the fear factor.

So what does this mean for Venus? What uncertainties are ahead for the planet of harmony and restoration? In Peter's case Venus sits at the crossover point from Virgo to Libra, its dignified rulership, and therefore a balance must be found between his *personalized* disillusion of life, whereby he must acquire a practical realization that the unknown may not necessarily represent a place of danger, hence trauma and tragedy—the Nodal signatures indented into the eighth house. This naturally links the twelfth house to the eighth via Neptune's sextile to Pluto and Neptune's quintile to Venus.

However, because Pluto in the twelfth is also debilitated (in its fall in Libra) this will be no easy task for Venus as these Nodal rulers are locked in a kind of power struggle. Pluto, whose nature it is to control, is reminding Venus that it is totally in control of the twelfth house and will adhere to the wishes of its brother Neptune indicated by the aforementioned sextile.[2] A sextile denotes an opportunity, but for what? In Peter's case that opportunity arrived in the form of escapism via the intoxicating and undeniable realm of alcoholism. That link between Pluto residing in the twelfth house of hidden fears and phobias and Neptune residing in the second house of self-esteem has played a key role in the onset of Peter's alcoholic tendencies.

The sign rulers of the Nodes, particularly Venus with its evolutionary quintile to Neptune, suggest that Peter's soul has perhaps carried this stigmatism over from past lives (twelfth house), coupled by Venus at twenty-nine degrees. Interestingly, Peter's drinking initially began as a need to socialize (Venus) but quickly developed into a defiant and relentless form of obsession with uncontrollable consequences (Pluto in the twelfth house). This is the classic chart of an alcoholic.

Conclusion

Because of the uncertainty generated by alcohol dependence, Peter's life is in a constant state of flux. He was fired from his job because of destruction of company property. He was involved in a serious automobile accident in a company car because he had been drinking heavily. Fortunately he wasn't injured and there were no other parties involved, but he received a suspended jail sentence and lost his licence (this occurred during Saturn's transiting square to its natal position). In addition, Peter's marriage has suffered a breakdown as a result of his continual drinking. Peter's future looks decisively uncertain and because of his "lack of trust" in people and establishments he continually refuses to seek help.

His refusal to seek help is also personified by the fact that most of his planets frequent the eastern side of the chart, so he is not easily convinced or persuaded to adopt a more flexible view of matters in hand. Furthermore, a common notion held by alcoholics is that they are in control of their drinking and can stop whenever they want to. This can be seen in Eric's chart in the first house Mercury-Uranus conjunction.

If Peter continues in this way he is likely to self-destruct.

Endnotes

[1] Information courtesy of Wikipedia.

²In ancient mythology Neptune and Pluto were brothers; they are also both water planets. This is an interesting concept considering the composition of alcohol is mostly water.

Alcohol Abuse

CHAPTER 13

Psychosis

PSYCHOSIS IS AN ABNORMAL CONDITION of the mind, and a psychiatric term for a mental state that is often described as involving a loss of contact with reality. People suffering from psychosis are described as *psychotic*. Psychosis is given to the more severe forms of psychiatric disorder, during which *hallucinations* and *delusions* and impaired insight may also occur.

The term psychosis is broad and can mean anything from relatively minor aberrant experiences to the complex and catatonic expressions of *schizophrenia* and bipolar disorder. Moreover, a wide variety of central nervous system diseases from both external substances and internal physiologic illness can produce symptoms of psychosis. This led many professionals to say that psychosis is not specific enough as a diagnostic term. Despite this, psychosis is generally given to noticeable deficits in normal behavior and more commonly to diverse forms of hallucinations or delusional beliefs (for example grandiosity and delusions of persecution). Someone exhibiting obvious signs could be described as psychotic, whereas one who is exhibiting subtle signs could be classified in the category of an attenuated psychotic risk syndrome.

In addition, people experiencing psychosis can exhibit personality changes and thought disorder. Depending on its severity, this may be accompanied by unusual behavior, as well as difficulty with social interaction and impairment in carrying out daily life exercises.[1]

Astrological Diagnosis

The Sun (ruler of the South Node's sign) is in relatively close proximity to the North Node in the sixth house of acute health matters in Elizabeth's chart. However, this conjunction strengthens the Sun's relationship to Uranus (ruler of the North Node's sign) via a semi-square to Venus and by Venus's square to Uranus. In most cases an aspect of this calibre would undermine the natural equilibrium of the objective mind, often causing psychological paralysis. Mercury, the old ruler of the sixth house, is also in this quadrant and square Saturn, further exacerbating the condition. Interestingly, the Moon at 1 Sagittarius is closely conjunct Neptune from Mercury's third house of communication; 1 Sagittarius is an Azimene degree.

The Moon-Neptune conjunction opposes the Mercury-ruled Midheaven, with the Moon ruling the eleventh house, the natural home of Uranus, and the ruler of the North Node's sign. Leo (ruler of the South Node's sign) also rules this domain with its majority influence encompassing the twelfth (Neptune's natural house, with Neptune being connected to the Moon). The Sun is square the Moon-Neptune configuration, and the Sun connects to Pluto in Virgo (Virgo being the archetypal ruler of the sixth) via an inconjunction, the aspect of adjustment. Pluto is at 29 Virgo in the first house of self. As previously discussed, twenty-nine degrees can often cast doubt and instill uncertainty. The Sun is debilitated in Aquarius (in detriment). Ordinarily, a debilitated Sun would increase the effects of any mental health condition, providing of course that there were other powerful factors in the chart.

Jupiter, in its dignity, also connects to the Moon via an applying conjunction, and Jupiter frequents the fourth house, the Moon's natural domain. The words from an old Marvin Gaye song, "wherever I lay my hat that's my home," is typical of this Moon-Jupiter configuration, and this is relevant to Elizabeth because she frequently attempts to create stability (Moon) while

Psychosis

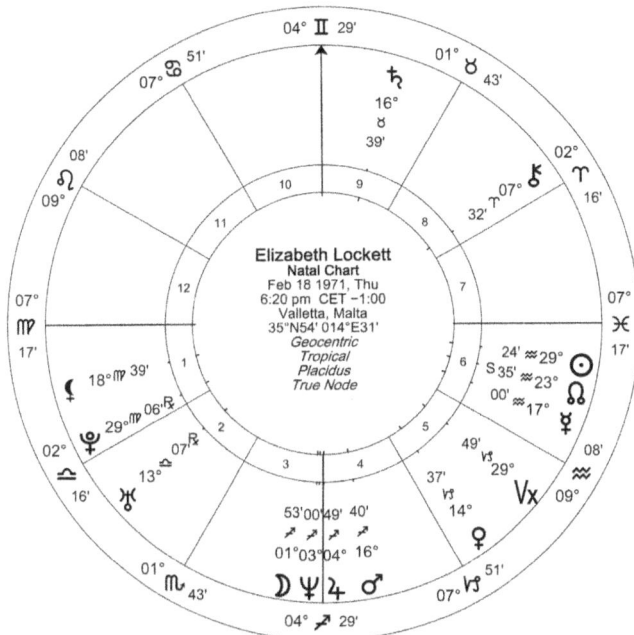

Elizabeth Lockett
Natal Chart
Feb 18 1971, Thu
6:20 pm CET −1:00
Valletta, Malta
35°N54' 014°E31'
Geocentric
Tropical
Placidus
True Node

being continually on the move (Jupiter). But because Jupiter has a tendency to promise more than it can actually deliver, which is reminiscent of its square to the Sun at twenty-nine degrees, stability is subject to frequent change (Moon-Jupiter-Neptune opposing the Gemini Midheaven).

According to the astrologer Alan Oken, Jupiter is the esoteric ruler of Aquarius (ruler of the North Node's sign).[2] Technically, the North Node has been *besieged* by the Sun and Mercury. I say "technically" because the Sun-Mercury conjunction to the North Node is wide. No more than one degree is generally the more accepted orb for planets that are traditionally said to be *besieged*. The effects of this North Node besiegement will also have consequences on the South Node in the twelfth house of unresolved matters of the heart, whereas the sixth house represents unresolved matters of the mind. So, in effect, the position of the Nodes coupled with Pluto's occupation of the first house will most definitely symbolize unfinished business.

In retrospect, Leo, the sign of the South Node, rules the heart chakra, and Aquarius, the sign of the North Node, co-rules the crown chakra with Libra (Uranus's accidental rulership sign). Algol occupies the ninth house, which oversees the nervous system and is also connected to the higher mind according to Alan Oken. Although the malign influence of this dark star does not administer its influence on the exact inconjunction from Mars to Saturn (the so-called malefic planets), its strenuous effects will nevertheless be experienced within the recesses of the mind, most likely causing extreme anxiety.

There is also a kind of three-way pyramid effect that emanates from the fourth, fifth, and sixth houses pointing to the ninth. This is clearly an important factor in the chart because it could hold the key to Elizabeth's financial future and well-being, especially because Venus in Capricorn and Saturn in Taurus are in mutual reception. Mercury's trine to Uranus could be partly responsible for fragility in the mind, which is often a factor in Elizabeth's life. Trines are not always beneficial, depending upon how they have been activated, consciously or unconsciously.[3]

Cancer co-rules the third eye chakra with Pisces (Neptune). Is it coincidental that these planets are conjunct? With this in mind, this is most definitely a chart that denotes powerful karmic connections!

If we remind ourselves again of the changeable effects reminiscent of psychosis we will be able to connect Neptune's position and affliction from the natural third house of Gemini opposing the Gemini Midheaven, and Mercury (the ruler of Gemini) to the *hallucination* and *delusion* factor, which are the main indications of the effects of this condition. It is a well known fact that Elizabeth persecutes herself and others through her grandiose desires and her completely *unreasonable* requests. In essence Neptune's influence here, especially in light of its closeness to the IC, would place this individual in a state of constant self-delusion. Due to Neptune's connection with the Sun (via a square) and its conjunction to Jupiter opposing the Midheaven, it would be responsible to suggest that this Sagittarius stellium with Neptune besieged is related to the onset of schizophrenia and bipolar disorder, additional illnesses that Elizabeth is known to suffer from.

This is most definitely a chart that portends of debilitating mental illness.

Prognosis

According to author Louise Hay, "psychosis occurs because there isn't enough trust placed on the natural process of life."

Elizabeth's chart denotes a clear need for *adjustment*. The exact inconjunction between Mars and Saturn with Mars ruling the eighth and Saturn ruling the fifth (the Sun's rulership house with the Sun accidentally ruling the twelfth and the home of the South Node) determines that the soul *cannot* and *must not* proceed down a similar path of self-undoing; it must, however, learn to *adjust* to a more conscious and practical way of life. Self-undoing was perhaps a key influence throughout past lives, whence the soul was lost in a psychotic maize of confusion, sobriety, and self-destruction, all of which are triggers for chronic psychosis.

Interestingly, when regressed under DMP the soul immediately returned to a specific incarnation and one where it had become deeply indented by the signature of a royal heritage (Leo South Node), meaning that Elizabeth had taken on a role as an important member of the royal aristocracy and one whom was warlike (self-destruction, self-undoing, dying needlessly in battle, Mars-Saturn inconjunction). Today this royalist echo reverberates through many areas of her life. Her function in this life is to adjust from that of the commander to the role of the humanitarian (healing her soul and the souls of others).

In order for the soul to reach its maximum potential a complete juxtaposition in evolutionary consciousness must occur.

Elizabeth's chart does highlight a multitude of positive opportunities for humanitarian advancement and growth. Personal growth is especially relevant via that three-way Nodal pyramid (Saturn at the apex of the pyramid and ruling the sixth), which points to the ninth house of direction, to which Jupiter also configures in the cosmic equation. However, there is a fine line that is forever being walked in this chart between sanity and insanity (the natural square between the sixth and ninth houses). It is possible that the three-way pyramid will orchestrate an enhanced form of psychosis, meaning that the affects of this illness would be greatly personified and hence multiplied to the extremes (Jupiter).

Essentially, transformation (meaning critical adjustment) is necessary and perhaps indicated in a psychological capacity by Chiron's position in the Mars-Pluto ruled eighth house. The orb difference between the eighth and the first house is 150 degrees, denoting the inconjunction aspect. Pluto's exact inconjunction to the Sun from the first to the sixth house means that the soul must find contentment through the order of service but not in a way that would be detrimental, meaning that the soul shouldn't acquire a heavy load and become weighted down by the issues of others.

Directing the soul toward humanitarian pursuits seems to be a recurring theme throughout the chart. The act of service must therefore be achieved through a desire to perform worthwhile causes that are beneficial to others. As with any illness, psychosis occurs when the soul finds itself at the wrong evolutionary juncture or on the wrong road that leads *away* from spiritual soul progression. Service to others is most definitely Elizabeth's route to soul progression.

Conclusion

Unfortunately, this story does not have a happy ending as Elizabeth is deeply entrenched in the effects of psychosis. She recently suffered from a complete mental and physical breakdown during the Uranus-Pluto square and its semi-sextile to transiting Saturn,[4] and the progressed Sun's opposition to progressed Uranus and the Ascendant, with Mars at the apex of a t-square in Capricorn (Saturn), and from the first, third, and sixth houses, which are primary houses in medical astrology. Another factor of this chart is that Elizabeth doesn't have any planet-to-planet oppositions; therefore, when confronted with delicate situations she can lack the art of diplomacy, which is another classic symptom psychosis.

Elizabeth *continues* to refuse treatment for this condition, often remarking that she has "nothing to say about it" and "it's everyone else's fault why she is this way"—a classic example of the hallucination and delusion factor of this illness. If she recognizes the symptoms of her condition and begins the healing process, adverse planetary influences will be an opportunity for enhanced soul growth.

This chart does suggest that Elizabeth was born with impaired mental abilities as indicated by the inconjunctions, and the likelihood of something like psychosis (the invisible demon of mental illness) manifesting at some point in her life was inevitable. Initially, the psychosis was diagnosed during a severe bout of biorhythm depletion. Two of the biorhythms that were low were the physical (ruled by Mars and Pluto) and mastery (ruled by the Sun, Jupiter, and Saturn). These planets represent the mental sensitive backdrop and thus the inconjunctions and the pyramid, which is the crux of the psychosis.

Endnotes

[1]Information courtesy of the *Medical Journal of Health and Well Being,* published by Collins.

[2]Information courtesy of *Soul Centred Astrology* by *Alan Oken.*

[3]In traditional and mundane astrology, trines are considered neutral aspects. However, in medical astrology trines are not al-

ways *favorable*.

[4]In my opinion semi-sextiles are similar to sesquiquadrates by which they give nuance to the saying, "the straw that broke the camel's back." Essentially, minor aspects represent the lighted fuse of the exploding time bomb, whereas major aspects represent the actual explosion.

CHAPTER 14

Breast Cancer

BREAST CANCER MOST COMMONLY ORIGINATES in the inner lining of the milk ducts, or the *lobules* that supply the ducts with milk. Cancers originating from ducts are known as *ductal carcinomas*, while those originating from lobules are known as *lobular carcinomas*. Breast cancer occurs in humans and other mammals. While the overwhelming majority of human cases occur in women, male breast cancer can also occur.

The characteristics of the cancer determine the treatment, which can include surgery, medication, hormonal therapy, chemotherapy, radiation, and/or immunotherapy. Worldwide, breast cancer accounts for 22.9 percent of all cancers in women. In 2008, breast cancer caused 458,503 deaths worldwide, equivalent to 13.7 percent of cancer deaths in women. Breast cancer is more than 100 times more common in women than in men, although men tend to have poorer outcomes due to delays in diagnosis.

Prognosis and survival rates for breast cancer vary greatly depending on the cancer type, stage, treatment, and geographical location of the patient. Survival rates in the Western world are high; for example, more than eight out of ten women (84 percent) in England diagnosed with breast cancer survive for at least five years. In developing countries, however, survival rates are much lower.[1]

Symptoms

The first noticeable and discernable symptom of breast cancer is typically a lump that feels *different* from the rest of the breast tissue. As a result more than 80 percent of breast cancer cases are discovered when the women feels the lump. The earliest breast cancers are detected by a *mammogram*. Lumps found in lymph nodes, located in the arm pits, can also indicate breast cancer.

Other indications of breast cancer, other than a lump, can include thickening in the breast tissue, meaning one breast becoming larger or lower; a nipple changing position or shape or becoming inverted, skin puckering or dimpling; a rash on or around a nipple; discharge from a nipple; constant pain in part of the breast or armpit; and sweating beneath the armpit or around the collarbone. Pain, however, known as mastodynia, is an *unreliable* tool in determining the presence of breast cancer, but may be indicative of other breast health issues.[2]

Astrological Diagnosis

Jayne's chart that *highlights* the impinging Moon-related illness of breast cancer.

If we start with the Nodes once again (the evolutionary centrepieces) we will begin to discern an unfolding pattern of health problems throughout this particular chart. But first it is important to understand at this stage that in order to bring about a balance of positive and negative energies, (the catalysts that will successfully *repel* illness and disease), a complete juxtaposition in consciousness must transpire at some point before the time of any affliction, which generally occurs via the onset of transiting planets. The Nodes are at 0 Gemini-Sagittarius in the third-ninth house polarity. Zero degrees signify undefined beginnings and potential trauma. The Nodes are in exaltation from these houses, making their personified influence ever more noticeable.

Meanwhile, the sign rulers of the Nodes (Mercury and Jupiter) are *debilitated* with Mercury in its fall in Pisces in the first

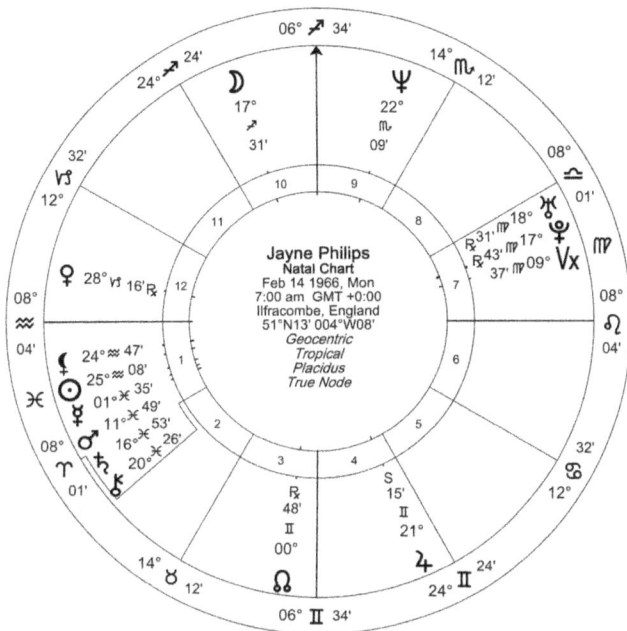

Jayne Philips
Natal Chart
Feb 14 1966, Mon
7:00 am GMT +0:00
Ilfracombe, England
51°N13' 004°W08'
Geocentric
Tropical
Placidus
True Node

house of the self, general health, and vitality. Jupiter is in detriment in Gemini in the fourth house of roots and the final journey; the fourth is the natural house of Cancer. The final journey or culminating cycle is also a Jupiter trait, depending on the level of soul progression attained. Cancer (ruling the breasts) rules the sixth house of health matters and the sixth house emphasizes the patient's particular illness or disease. Jupiter opposes the Moon (ruler of the sixth) within a four-degree applying aspect, so the combined effects of these planets will reverberate via the sixth house of health.

Moreover, the Moon and Jupiter form a significant part of a Grand Cross configuration with Saturn, Uranus, and Pluto. Saturn also rules the twelfth house of death, karma, and hospitalization (essentially hospitals are institutions that tend to the effects of chronic-based illness). The Sun and Mercury are square the Nodes with Mercury ruling the North Node's sign, and the

One Body Many Illnesses   145

Sun and Mercury are at the apex of the Nodal polarity that symbolizes a t-square. The Sun is also debilitated (in detriment) in Aquarius, weakening the effects of the Nodes at zero degrees.

From this brief planetary outline with Cancer as the primary archetype we can formulate the kind of illness that is likely to ensue, especially when we note the Moon (the ruler of Cancer) is at 17 Sagittarius 31, or twenty-nine minutes from an Azimene Degree, which is 18 Sagittarius. In retrospect we could theorize that the natal orb declination of the Moon would naturally indicate a flaw or disposition within the Cancer archetype, which will affect the sixth and twelfth house polarity and all that it stands for. With so much emphasis on the Cancer-Capricorn archetypes only a specific kind of illness or disease is showcased by these signs and their rulers, which greatly influence the South Node sign ruler. This close-nit effect would personify the self-induced clauses of *trauma* and *tragedy*, traits that are traditionally associated with the lunar Nodes.

In addition, Venus at 28 Capricorn in the twelfth house is also an Azimene Degree. Venus's semi-square to Mars in Pisces (leaky energy) weakens the solidity of the Capricorn archetype and the first house, indicating that the individual is highly susceptible to disease. The first house has been further debilitated by the conjunction of Mars and Saturn, Saturn being the ruler of the twelfth from both Capricorn and Aquarius.

Another theme here is unfinished business as indicated by Pluto square the Moon and opposition from the seventh house. Pluto, Uranus, and Saturn are intercepted, and Saturn and Uranus rule the twelfth house of karma. It is conceivable that Jayne suffered from breast cancer in a previous life, and therefore it is likely that she may have failed to attain a healthy equilibrium in the body that would have helped to stave off this chronic and debilitating condition. Failing to acquire harmony (Venus) could also have been a contributing factor, as it remains so in the present incarnation.

Furthermore, Jayne has a low opinion of herself, and her self-worth is in a constant state of flux (Saturn's opposition to Pluto from the first and is intercepted). She also finds it difficult to embrace her most natural, introspective, and cherished human gift: learning to love herself and life. This is indicated by the Sun, which rules the heart chakra, square Neptune from Jupiter's South Node domain of the ninth, and square the North Node of potential tragedy.[3] As indicated in Chapter 4, refusing to love oneself, especially where women are concerned, is a major cause of breast cancer.

Both her Nodes rule the throat chakra, which denotes *self-expression*, and expression has been another key area for concern in her life. Self-expression is a factor easily denoted by the stellium in the first house. The planetary stellium is also disposed by the isolated presence of Mercury from this domain. There are only two aspects from Mercury to other planets, which are the Sun and Moon, the luminaries, and they are wide aspects that pack little punch; so the planet of communication may feel somewhat cut off from the rest of the cosmos. Therefore, as Mercury is designated as the cosmos's messenger, maybe he is finding it difficult to honor his chosen role and instead is being rebuffed by the Gods. After all, Pisces and Sagittarius are the signs that traditionally symbolize the hierarchy of the Gods.

Jayne has a tendency to be *misunderstood*, and at times she can be *ignored* by others, almost to the point that she doesn't seem to exist (the Pisces stellium linked to foggy Neptune). Consequently, these emotionally-oriented issues frequently cause discord and strife in her life and may have assisted in the onset of disease (aided by the Mars-Saturn first house conjunction).

Jayne was diagnosed with breast cancer in 2008, during Saturn's transiting opposition to its natal position conjoining Uranus and Pluto in the Venus-Black Moon Lilith ruled seventh house, and square Jupiter and the Moon, thus disposing the Nodes. Unfortunately, in 2011, she was also diagnosed with emphysema during transiting Neptune's transit of Pisces (signifying wasting illness). Neptune conjoined Mercury (North Node sign ruler) and was square the Nodes. The lungs come under the jurisdiction of the throat chakra, which partly rules the third along with the North Node, and the third house rules the lungs. Transiting Saturn was also moving through the eighth and in a square with Venus at the time of diagnosis. At this point she was admitted to hospital for treatment. Chemotherapy had catastrophic effects on the body (Uranus in Pisces in the first house opposing natal Uranus and Pluto conjoining Saturn and Chiron).

Prognosis

According to author Louise Hay, "breast cancer occurs because of a refusal to nourish oneself; and instead there is a tendency to put everyone else first."

Breast cancer is essentially a tumor that forms in the breast. There has been much speculation and a varying difference of opinion over the years as to which planet rules *tumors*. As a tumor will in most cases expand in size, especially when left untreated, tumors must therefore come under the rulership of Jupiter (ruler of the South Node's sign), which is associated with multiplication, a trait of cancer cells. Jupiter also rules warts and other such growths that are void of fluid. Abscesses and boils (containing poisonous fluid or puss) come under the rulership of Pluto, as these types of growths emulate the volcanic effect with puss rising to the surface like magma.

Initially, tumors can form when changes in the blood particles (or cells) occur, meaning that a tumor can often be the result of a blood disorder or an imbalance that occurs in the blood cells. So, for example, a disease that destroys the red blood cells, which would invariably leave an overabundance of white blood cells, could lead to the formation of a tumor in a particularly vulnerable part of the body—a malady that is most certainly connected to Jupiter.

As natal Jupiter is in Gemini (its dispositional sign), blood disorders could be an initial factor to consider. When Jayne was growing up she was diagnosed with leukaemia, a disease defined by an abnormal proliferation of white blood cells that affects the bone marrow. These abnormal white blood cells can also affect the nervous system (Mercury ruler of the North Node's sign). Although she made a complete recovery, this disease will have dire consequences in later life (Saturn).

Meanwhile, the Moon can also act as the *conveyor* and *distributor* of illness, especially when located in hard aspect to Jupiter, whose purpose is to *expand* and thus multiply everything it contacts. According to author Heinrich Daath, the Moon can also be associated with tumours.[4] The Moon's square to Mars can be indicative of defective red blood particles. As the Moon oversees the breasts, a blood disorder might have been the initial cause of the breast cancer because the chart does seem to suggest this possibility. This is indicative of the Moon's opposition to *Jupiter*, and *Mercury's* square to the Nodes—the starting points for illness.

Conclusion

Jayne died in 2012. Death seemed an almost inevitable factor, especially when Jupiter (the final journey) began crossing the North Node in the third house and formed an inconjunction with transiting Saturn from the eighth house of death and with Pluto in the eleventh. A Yod (finger of God) aspect had formed as Saturn and Pluto were sextile. Neptune had also conjoined Mercury and was square the Nodes. Ironically, Jayne *didn't* die from breast cancer, but instead died from emphysema (third house of lungs).

Each of us has installed within the psyche a physical and spiritual time reference, which is ruled by Saturn and Neptune. This time reference is our cue to go, to leave our mortal bodies and traverse toward a greater endeavor or purpose. For Jayne the

Finger of God, which was connected to the Nodes via Mercury and Jupiter, was pointing toward the final phase of her life (the fourth house). So, just as we make our grand entrance via the Ascendant and the fourth house, we must too make our grand finale via the influence of the Ascendant and the fourth house, which is traditionally ruled by the Moon and her ecliptic points: the Nodes.

It has been proven that mushrooms strengthen the immune system and thus protect us against illness and disease. It is also believed that the regular consumption of mushrooms guards against breast cancer in women. Mushrooms and other forms of fungi come under the jurisdiction of Pluto. If Pluto is strongly emphasized in the birth chart it is an indication of a flaw or weakness in the immune system, and therefore consuming mushrooms on a regular basis would decrease the likelihood of illness.[5] Jayne rarely ate mushrooms.

Endnotes

[1] Information source for medical statistics: *Wikipedia*.

[2] Information courtesy of the *Medical Encyclopaedia of Health and Well Being,* published by Collins.

[3] It is important to stipulate here that trauma and tragedy are not necessarily occurrences that manifest solely in a physical capacity. As Jayne's Nodes frequent cognitive signs trauma and tragedy are most likely to manifest in a mental/psychologically-orientated capacity.

[4] The Moon's association with tumors taken from *Heinrich Daath's* publication *Medical Astrology* originally published in 1914 by *Fowlers and Co* of London.

[5] For more information on the health benefits of mushrooms and indeed other nutritional factors I highly recommend: www.mercola.com.

CHAPTER 15

Conclusion

HIPPOCRATES, THE FATHER OF MEDICINE, wrote in his diaries, "he who practices medicine without the benefit of the movement of the stars and the planets is a fool." According to Hippocrates, and as proven repeatedly in modern-day surgery, "disobeying this cosmic law will invariably result in one of three failures of any surgery performed at the wrong time: 1) complications, 2) unusually slow and painful healing and recuperation, and 3) fatality."

It is reassuring to know that there are discernable points in the heavens (cosmic beacons) that offer spiritual and evolutionary guidance. But unfortunately the polarized magnetic influence of these celestial positions is often presented to us through the misconceived eyes and ears of adversity: the Moon's North and South Nodes.

Jyotish and Hindu astrology believe the Nodes to be *malefic*; these ancient teachings also consider them to be the most powerful points in the natal chart. To some degree I agree with this hypothesis, especially when it comes to determining potential illness in the chart and, as we have learned, my method of analysis can be successfully accentuated through the premise of *Nodal Chart Interpretation*. In addition, I believe the Nodes hold a significant evolutionary purpose for us to discover and thus embrace; however in order to accomplish this we must let go of our inhibitions and fears. But, as author Ivy Goldstein Jacobson emphasises, the Nodes can also be the catalyst for *trauma* and *tragedy*.

Trauma and tragedy are issues that are purely dependent upon the nature and the severity of the unfolding life changes that come our way from time to time—those *unknown* and *unfamiliar* forces that are associated with long-term change. It is important to stipulate that trauma and tragedy only exist because of the absence of love and true heartfelt faith in the world. Instead, human nature has become fearful of what it doesn't understand or conceive, and long-term change is one of our *ultimate* fears. No longer do we perceive change to mean adventure; we prefer to see it as a major burden.[1] All illnesses can be purged through the acceptance of the light.

Furthermore, if we allow the forces of trauma and tragedy to transmute psychologically, they can often become the terrifying demons that Jyotish teachings believe the Nodes to be representative of, thus symbolizing the head and tail of the dragon or serpent. But the Nodes do *not* have to be the instruments of discord and displeasure, and even death (as in "giving up with life" in a psychological way, which is the basis for mental illness). Alternatively, the energy of the Nodes can be transcended, whereby they can become pointers for harmonic transformation, spiritual rebirth and stoic realization.

Meanwhile, it is reasonable to suggest that the effects of the Nodes are anything but mundane; instead, they tend to operate in a psychological capacity. This is perhaps why the Nodes have the potential to symbolize our inner demons, especially as they can highlight that margin of error (unfinished business) with which we frequently reincarnate.

Following a true spiritual path is far from easy, especially in this materialistic world of endless distractions, mundane repetition, and sublime illusion. But that is where the chart's cosmic potential of planetary interplay can assist in our constant search for the truth and divine solidarity. Once we learn to expedite the purpose of the Nodes, the effects can be truly beneficial to our spiritual direction and evolutionary progression. This is assuming we understand that the Nodes are not compatible with the physical plane in any way, thereby making it difficult to fully comprehend the effects of their mystical powers and temperamental energies. Similar to most things that defy the modern laws of physics, the Nodes have been entrenched by so many definitions.

As a result many people believe that eclipses hold some special and significant message that is once again misinterpreted in a physical capacity. Spiritual progression and evolutionary transcendence are therefore the true purpose and function of the Nodes.

Illness and disease often occur when we lose sight of our inherent purpose, hence our way in life, and more importantly our journey upon the evolutionary ladder of realization and remembrance. The Nodes represent our internal compass, but if we find ourselves in the wrong place at the wrong time our compass will malfunction, or to put it another way it will simply go *haywire*, pointing us in all directions, except the right one. To tread a spiritual path we need to trust the guidance of our internal compass; once we embrace this realization the concepts of trauma and tragedy will cease to exist, even poor health begins to improve.

Immense change (evolutionary transformation) is often associated with trauma and tragedy. When the thread of life breaks because too much strain is applied, it is inadvertently replaced by a wholly new thread to which its fibres are bound by uncertainty. When this occurs it is considered to be traumatic and a tragedy. Changes of this magnitude occur at certain times in life when transiting planets affect the Nodes via hard aspects, especially Saturn, Uranus, Neptune and Pluto. Saturn is probably considered to be *unrelenting* in its approach to Nodal transformation, meaning that Saturn transits of the Nodes are never easy affairs. Saturn does, however, crystalize our inner child, or at least has the potential to do so, until such time that Jupiter releases it. Illness and disease feed on these probabilities, and Saturn (like Mars and Pluto) doesn't hold back so to speak when it comes to instigating illness and disease.

Under such times of great planetary stress the Nodes will often be considered as malign influences. But if change is perceived rather as spiritual and evolutionary progression, hence the reintegration of the negative (South Node) and the positive (North Node) energies, the Nodes would be considered as the potential they truly represent: points in the heavens that denote spiritual and evolutionary guidance—universal beacons of hope.

Using the simple premise of *Nodal Chart Interpretation* will not only offer up the opportunity to ascertain forthcoming illness and disease but it will also allow us to rediscover the true purpose of our life on Earth—our evolutionary heritage and insight into a greater creative expression. Understanding the sublime cosmic interplay we call *astrology* will help us to understand ourselves!

The Purpose of the Luminaries

The Sun and the Moon (the luminaries) present the greatest potential for spiritual and evolutionary progression—the Sun overseeing the chakras (the soul's energy points) and the Moon with her biorhythms (the Soul's heartbeats), and the Nodes. Interpreting a chart using this integrated and personalized formula (chakras, biorhythms and the Nodes), it is possible to build up a viable picture of the life plan with all its challenges and opportunities. Biorhythm interpretation is particularly helpful to understanding the outcome of illness and disease. For example, in medical astrology biorhythms can be most effectual in the chart when influenced by the Moon's primary phases, which are:

The New Moon. This phase implies biorhythm disintegration, transformation and preparation for a new cycle of growth. The New Moon is the low ebb, the systole. During this phase at least one of the primary biorhythms will be below the midline.

The First Quarter. This phase is concerned with organic development and the revitalisation of function and fluid.

The Full Moon. This typifies fruition, maturation, extreme tension, and fluid plenitude. This phase is the lunar expiration and diastole. During this phase at least one primary biorhythm will be above the midline.

The Final Quarter. This is devoted to the application of power already generated by The Full Moon. The medullar and cerebral substances are augmented at The Full Moon and suffers diminution at The New Moon.

The New and Full Moon phases are particularly relevant to the movements of the three primary rhythms, whereas the Quarterly phases are particularly relevant to the movements of the seven secondary rhythms. Always check biorhythm activity in the chart during these particular phases of the Moon. Moreover, check the transiting Nodes and their affects on the biorhythms via the transiting Nodal rulers.

Simply by synergizing the Sun's chakras, the Moon's biorhythms, and the Moon's Nodes we will develop a far greater understanding of the medical and evolutionary condition and purpose of the natal chart.

Unfortunately, there are no solutions at the physical level to the problems that we continue to endure upon this planet. The answers will only transpire when we change our way of thinking. In order to save ourselves and our planet Earth before it's too late, we need to learn to think from the heart-mind as opposed to the head-mind. The issues of despair and degradation that are prevalent throughout the world are occurring because of the consequences created by the way we think. In essence we have *forgotten* our spiritual heritage and therefore we have disassociated ourselves from the divine.

Endnote

[1]Mahatma Gandhi said, "we haven't come to Earth to settle down, life is an on-going adventure, only fools become complacent."

About the Author

Alan R.Wheatcroft BA, DMS.ASTROL has studied astrology since his first Saturn return; and now works primarily as an evolutionary and medical astrologer. Alan also runs a spiritual healing center in the UK, which helps people overcome trauma, and teaches the appropriate meditations and techniques to those who wish to raise their soul's spiritual vibration. He is also involved with The Band of Light (references to this organization and its incredible work are displayed at different points throughout the book).

In addition, Alan is often invited to speak at universities, colleges, business organizations and spiritual groups with regards to the importance of astrology and why this ancient discipline can be the universal key that opens the vault revealing spiritual insight and knowledge—essential elements for spiritual progression.

A successful writer, Alan has been published throughout the professional and popular media. He is also a regular contributor to Wanda Sellar's *Astrology and Medicine* newsletter (available via The Astrological Association). *One Body Many Illnesses: An Insightful Approach to Medical Astrology* is Alan's first major publication.

Alan can be reached at: alanrichards59@gmail.com

"Medical Astrology is a popular subject with several books available on Amazon and many websites dedicated to the art. It is hugely complicated though. Looking at a person's birth information, when referring to the planetary/star/moons/houses/alignments, etc. can lead to the root cause of a person's illness.

"Alan says his book is unique because he uses spiritual influences to determine the root core of illness. He also provides a full natal chart which clearly highlights the potential source of illness and disease, thus making medical diagnosis quicker because the practitioner knows where the weaknesses lie based on the individual's chart.

"It is a very interesting and well researched piece of work that many advanced astrologers and people with an interest can use. This is an alternative method of looking at why people become ill, and more important, how to see where the weaknesses lie, and take measures to prevent illnesses from even happening. I can definitely see its worth."—Steven Kayne, Chief Editor, Saltire Books

www.ingramcontent.com/pod-product-compliance
Lightning Source LLC
Chambersburg PA
CBHW021402090426
42742CB00009B/974